THE LIFE AND TIMES OF LA MERI

The Queen of Ethnic Dance

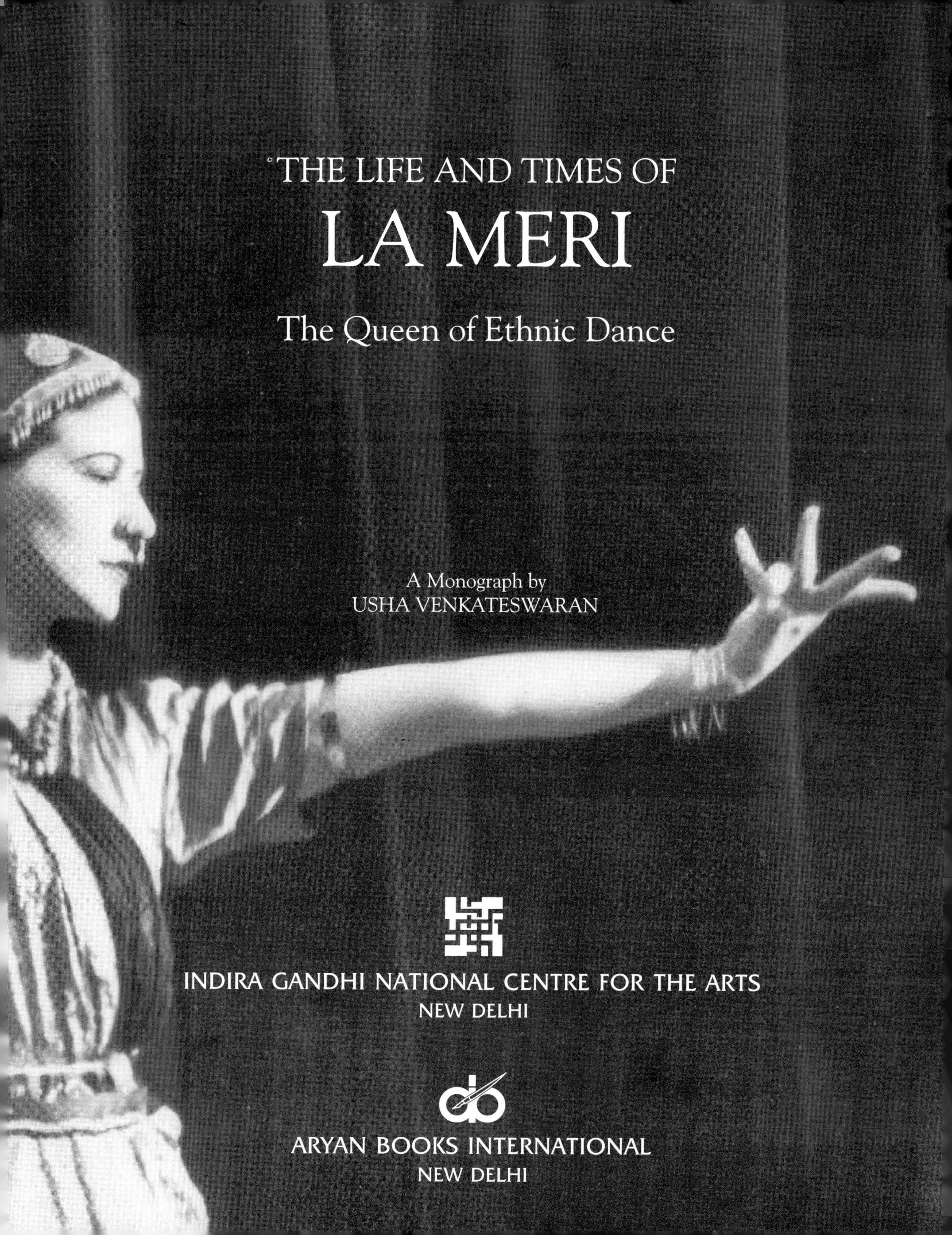

THE LIFE AND TIMES OF LA MERI

The Queen of Ethnic Dance

A Monograph by
USHA VENKATESWARAN

INDIRA GANDHI NATIONAL CENTRE FOR THE ARTS
NEW DELHI

ARYAN BOOKS INTERNATIONAL
NEW DELHI

THE LIFE AND TIMES OF LA MERI
The Queen of Ethnic Dance

ISBN-81-7305-292-1

First Published in 2005 by
INDIRA GANDHI NATIONAL CENTRE FOR THE ARTS
Central Vista Mess, Janpath, New Delhi - 110 001 (India)
and
ARYAN BOOKS INTERNATIONAL
Pooja Apartments, 4B, Ansari Road, New Delhi - 110 002 (India)
Tel. : 23287589, 23255799; Fax : 91-11-23270385; E-mail aryanbooks@vsnl.com

Cover & Layout design by Kamal P. Jammual
Computer Typeset at ABI Prints & Publishing Co., New Delhi
Printed in India at B.B.N. Printers, New Delhi

Foreword

People say that Indian classical dance is ancient, they also say that it has had an unbroken continuity. True, very true, but not all true. Whatever we see of Indian classical dance, which elsewhere I have given the appellation of the neoclassical dance, was indeed a conscious re-construct of a tradition. Its history is young and short. Many movements were responsible for the emergence of this re-construct. There were many people who contributed. The history is complex and intricate. The zig-zag road of the socio-economic-political, the textual, the historical, the theoretical and the practical, the national and the international, the Indian and the foreign, the experience and the represented visible, is hidden under the surface of a smooth and enchanting performance which appears to flow with silken liquidity. Once this surface is scratched or the shell opened, then all the intricate elements of an yet unresolved zig-zag puzzle of the creation of a classicity which is contemporary and not ancient begin to surface.

One amongst these important constituents is the connection of the national and international, the Indian and the foreign, the home and the abroad. The chance but fateful encounter of Anna Pavlova and Rukmini Devi, or more closely of Anna Pavlova and Uday Shankar, set in motion trajectories of exploration in different directions and different levels. It is difficult although not impossible to imagine what would have happened to contemporary classical or modern dance in the absence of this seminal and other such encounters. Would Rukmini Devi have turned her gaze inward to the recesses of the tradition to rejuvenate? Would an Uday Shankar have remained a painter or a musician? Would he have heralded a movement called 'modern dance' in India? But these fascinatingly inviting forays into speculation of possibilities and probabilities have been undertaken by some, alas not with the insightful rigour required to juxtapose the socio-political, economic, intellectual and artistic, even to hypothesize.

Our story in the pages of this monograph is different, but not unconnected. Almost concurrently with the arousing of the insatiable curiosity and discovery of the wealth which lay behind the 'surface' dimmed with dust of socio-cultural discourse of the twenties and thirties, were the courageous, artistic, adventures of a generation of American dancers. The story of Ruth St Denis is well-known and her response to Indian dance well documented, but La Meri, the younger, no less adventurous and yet more painstaking and serious, was indeed the first to lay the foundations of the first serious school of a systemized training of Indian dance, specially Bharatanatyam. No longer was it an impressionistic reconstruction of a mysterious Orient through a kinetic vocabulary totally alien to the East. Instead, it was a purposive and painstaking attempt to understand and analyze another vocabulary of body language and kinesthetics. She succeeded admirably. For her, it was the experienced body and not representation of the other, clothed with sinuous flowing garments. Although there is a sizeable body of archival material relating to La Meri at the Lincoln Centre, the critical writing and evaluation of her work is meagre, almost scanty. Conscious of this, I was excited at the prospect of acquiring La Meri's diaries and other memorabilia.

I had visited La Meri's studio in the late forties, and had kept in touch with her intermittently. I always sat quietly watching, not commenting, or even letting know of my own involvement with dance. The recollection of these visits, her elegant presence, and the memory of her imparting training to her students are altogether too vivid.

Thus, when by chance in my hunt for material of an archival nature, I came upon the notice of her private diaries being available for acquiring, I jumped at the opportunity. It was too good to be true.

I wasted not a single minute. I knew that the material would contain most valuable and revealing information. I was aware of her adventurous stormy life, also her total devotion and dedication to dance of all lands and cultures, but especially Indian. Somewhere the soul of India had touched her. I did succeed in acquiring this material for the archives of the Indira Gandhi National Centre for the Arts. The material was fascinating, specially her diary and letters. Archival material is a precious possession of any library, but it must be made available to a larger public. It was important that the material be made available in a readable form for all those interested in La Meri and in the history as also historiography of the revival and re-establishment of Indian dance in the third and fourth decades of the century.

Naturally despite the temptation of attempting this myself as a scholar, I requested Usha Venkateswaran to undertake the arduous task of going through the collections of her memorabilia—diary, letters, articles—and prepare a monograph.

Ushaji has done a most commendable job in preparing a monograph on the basis of this memorabilia, which is precise, insightful and meaningful. She has divided her material with great care and sensitivity. These six chapters—Looking through a Mirror: a Glimpse of Personal Life; Images: La Meri and the Indian Imagery; Crystals: La Meri as an Ethnic Dance Expert; Reflections: Inspirations and Achievements; Spotlight: Stars on and off the Stage; and Rainbow: The Colourful Life and Beyond—illustrate different facets of this colourful personality.

Usha Venkateswaran deftly reconstructs La Meri's life from the material in the IGNCA's archives. Even from this limited corpus, it is clear that La Meri was passionate about and committed to exploring different cultures through her own body. It is an astonishing feat for anyone to learn and far more to master diverse kinetic vocabularies. This she did with a rare sense of seriousness and sincerity. But from amongst all these voyages of dance vocabularies, it was the Indian that held her attention most. Her book, *Gesture Language of the Hindu Dance,* was a first attempt to document *hasta's.* The fact that there are some inaccuracies does not diminish the importance of the book as a milestone in the trajectory of comprehending movement, analytically. *The Technique of Hindu Dance* was a pedagogic exercise to assist students. Her line drawings were an equally innovative method of communicating the very distinctive ways of using the spine in different ethnic dances. It will be recalled that at that time no attempt had been made to notate Indian dance either through Banesh or Laban system.

The monograph allows the reader to peep into her personal life and her dancing colleagues and partners. The complex relationship with Ram Gopal will no doubt interest readers.

The photographs bear testimony to the versatility of La Meri the artist, La Meri the woman. The artist and the teacher played different roles in life, as she did on stage—and not a dull moment. I have no doubt that it will add significantly to the meagre literature on the extraordinary self made artist. She is an important link in the quest for reconstructing and reassembly of the parts to make a new whole.

The monograph has been awaiting publication for some time. I am glad that IGNCA has now decided to publish it. I would like to place on record my deep appreciation of Smt. Usha Venkateswaran's sincerity and understanding and for responding to my request. Usha Venkateswaran brings to the monograph her own mature comprehension of movement vocabularies as one trained in both Bharatanatyam and Ballet, and her sensitivity as a scholar.

April 19, 2004 **Kapila Vatsyayan**

Preface

The twentieth century has produced many talented dancers and teachers who have been eulogised for their skills. The period between 1920 and 1940 was rich with cultural awakening and interaction in the field of dance.

In Europe and America, ballet schools became well established and teachers came from different countries to enrich the art by learning as well as lending their skills and creating cross-cultural influences. Dancers moved from one country to the other and gave performances. Individual creativity of some great dancers like Anna Pavlova, Isadora Duncan, Martha Graham, Charles and Mary Wigman and Ruth St. Denis dramatically changed the trends, creating immense excitement.

There was a spurt of interest in the dances of the Orient and all the creative dancers in the West adapted various aspects from this rich heritage which suited their taste and aptitude. Those who came to India went back with their own impressions of the dance forms. Some called it the 'Hindu dance' and others 'Nautch'.

India, under British colonial rule, was prevented from freely practising her traditional art forms, especially the temple dances, performed by the devadasis as an offering to God. In fact, the devadasi tradition too was banned by the British and masses were thereby denied the opportunity of seeing these dances being performed. Fortunately, this art was kept alive by the dedicated and diligent Nattuvanars, the hereditary teachers of traditional dance and by the devadasis within their family circles.

It was during this period that Anna Pavlova, Ruth St. Denis and La Meri visited India. Pavlova was greatly impressed by the spiritual quality of these dances and introduced them in her ballet. She also invited Uday Shankar to dance with her and be a part of her troupe. It was Uday Shankar who helped her to understand and present the Indian dance.

Ruth St. Denis visited India in 1926 with Ted Shawn and she succeeded in capturing some of the impressions and the essence of the country, which she interpreted in her own way. Her dance pieces, *Sari dance*, *Incense*, etc., were simple but exotic for the American audiences and were very popular for a limited period of time.

Ten years after Ruth St. Denis, La Meri burst upon the scene with her visit to India. One may well say that, 'She came; she saw; and she conquered!'. Inspired by Uday Shankar's dance in Paris, she was eager to come to India. She was fortunate to see Bhanumathi and Varalakshmi perform Bharatanatyam at the very beginning of her stay. She was able to persuade their dance teacher, Guru Papanasam Vadivelu Pillai, to teach her this difficult art form. The credit goes to La Meri for learning Bharatanatyam with commendable diligence, determination and devotion in a short period of time, so much so that she was in a position to give a performance in Madras, along with Bhanumathi and Varalakshmi within three months. Thereafter, she studied Kathak under Ram Dutt Misra in Lucknow and recorded the music for the dances in Calcutta to take back with her.

In doing so, La Meri made an immense contribution, since she used the music for her performances and later started the School of Natya to teach Indian dance to her American students. Indian dance was thus performed by foreigners outside India, coinciding with the revival of traditional Indian dances by Balasaraswathi and Rukmini Arundale within India.

When I visited the United States in 1986 regarding the Festival of India, I was very impressed by the numerous dancers and dance teachers who talked to me about La Meri and her efforts to popularise and teach 'Hindu dance' there. I met Matteo who had worked with La Meri and revived her original production of *Swan Lake* in the Bharatanatyam style. A filmstrip of this production which I saw, was most impressive. There could not be a better illustration of cross-cultural fertilisation through dance.

So, when Dr Kapila Vatsyayan told me about the collection of her memorabilia acquired by the Indira Gandhi National Centre for the Arts and asked me whether I would be interested in working on it, I was thrilled and accepted straightaway. I decided to work on the La Meri collection as I was drawn by the sincerity of her responses and her single-minded pursuit of dance as a major contributor to universal human understanding. I have since then studied the available material and also talked to various people in India and the USA who have been associated with La Meri and her work, to arrive at an objective appraisal of her life and achievements.

I would like to thank Dr Kapila Vatsyayan for giving me this opportunity and also her valuable advise at various stages of this book.

I also extend my sincere thanks to Dr K.K. Chakravarty, Member-Secretary, IGNCA, for making the publication of this volume possible.

My thanks are also due to Dr L.M. Gujral, former Hony. Advisor, IGNCA, for the help rendered in publishing this book and Mr A.P. Gakhar for providing me adequate facilities to do my research in the IGNCA Library. I would also like to thank Dr (Mrs.) Advaitavadini Kaul, Editor, Kalakosha, IGNCA, for her editorial suggestions and seeing the volume through the press.

I feel La Meri's work has not ended and hope it can help to perpetuate her goals, not only in America but also in other parts of the world, including India.

Usha Venkateswaran

Contents

Introduction

Even before language was born, human beings communicated through movements and gestures, which later evolved into rituals and ceremonies.

Born in America, La Meri went through a gamut of activities and finally focused on dance—classical ballet, modern dance, Spanish dance, etc., gave many concerts and worked her way up to be recognised as a solo concert artiste. In India, La Meri, in her own words, 'began to find new strength within myself, fresh faith in my own capabilities'. After seeing her performances in India, the romantics declared her to be a reincarnation of an *apsara*, while the more down-to-earth said her coming was a milestone in Indian art.

Long before La Meri's visit in 1926, Ruth St. Denis and Ted Shawn performed in India. There were rave reviews of their programmes in different cities. It is presumed that Ruth St. Denis's non-authentic Indian dance helped to reawaken the slumbering art of dance in India. Pavlova's visit to India, the year after, created a stir and she inspired Rukmini Arundale to study Bharatanatyam seriously and start 'Kalakshetra', the renowned school of dance in Madras. Earlier Pavlova had also selected Uday Shankar to dance with her and this opened a new vista for Indian contemporary dances. No doubt nautch girls and their popular dancing were extant, but there was too little understanding of and exposure to the classical, sophisticated dance forms of India.

Therefore it was a great step forward when La Meri came to India in 1936 and learnt Bharatanatyam and Kathak.

In the short time, she learnt Bharatanatyam from excellent teachers—Guru Papanasam Vadivelu Pillai and Gauri Ammal—and even gave a public performance in the famous Museum Theatre in Madras, winning applause from the discerning audience. She went to Lucknow and learnt Kathak from Ram Dutt Misra and gave fifteen concerts in seven cities of India. She managed to get musicians to compose music for her dances and recorded it. Not a moment was wasted.

The best part was that she was able to perform these dances in India during her stay and went back to her country with these acquired treasures.

La Meri toured and performed in different corners of the world. She simultaneously learnt the local dances and imbibed their cultural content, later adding them to her repertoire. So Indian dance was performed in Columbia, Spanish dance in Japan, Hawaiian dance in Morocco, etc. Most of all, she worked very hard on these dances, till she mastered them well enough to earn the approval of the experts. Her reputation as an excellent Spanish dancer was well deserved and her book, *The Spanish Dance* is a classic, which is still studied seriously by students. Once, even Anna Pavlova asked La Meri to see her perform the Spanish Mexican dance to satisfy herself that it was as good as it was reputed to be.

She was a prolific writer too and had an attractive and expressive way of writing. She wrote newsy letters to her sister Lilian. In early years of her marriage to Guido Carreras, she composed poems in each of her letters, expressing her deepest feelings. She also wrote five volumes of poetry.

The La Meri collection of her memorabilia at IGNCA contains : (1) Diary of notes; (2) Letters to her sister Lilian and husband Guido Carreras; (3) Teaching notes; (4) Choreographic notes; (5) Details of her courses; (6) Letters from other friends; (7) Her notations on other artistes; (8) Some articles on dance related topics; (9) Pieces of fiction written rather humorously; (10) A big collection of photographs portraying her life and dance activities; (11) A few books written by her, including the unedited manuscript of her autobiography, which reveals her ability to capture every detail and express it jauntily and with frankness; (13) Audio cassettes which are a confirmation of her warmth and sincerity when she spoke at the award giving ceremonies; (14) A few filmstrips of her and the Natya group performing. One could see in all this her flair for choreography, stage composition and costume design.

In her own words, "There is still so much I want to do. I want to gather all I know of ethnic dance into one big volume prodigally using my millions of notes on the subject. I want to continue to help new young dancers to carry on the work of bringing the aesthetic wisdom of the older dance arts to the enrichment of America and I want to make aware of the young artistes, works".

She, in search of her quest, had to overcome many hurdles though often she writes about them flippantly. One can deduce how hard she tried to move from one stage to the other, changing tactics, adapting to the circumstances, but persevering her main goal. She literally drove through the snowstorm for her lecture demonstrations with students, worked eleven hours without a break, borrowed money from her sister to run courses and invested all her father's inheritance in supporting her dance academy and jeopardised her own health by performing while running a high fever.

In the present monograph, La Meri's own words have been quoted wherever possible, so that she speaks for herself directly and readers can more fully appreciate her personality. She was engagingly direct and friendly, but not an extrovert. In fact she was slightly shy and never flashy. Above all, she was a patriotic American who understood human nature and so could appreciate different cultures and art forms. She had the sensitivity to perceive the potential that these art forms had for enriching the minds of people, thereby bringing about a better understanding conducive for fostering friendship. She was not successful in earning the name of a 'great dancer' like Anna Pavlova or Isadora Duncan. But neither did others earn the well deserved name that La Meri did, of being the 'Queen of Ethnic Dance'. She not only could transform herself into nearly thirty different nationalities in their distinctive dance styles and costumes, but she also did that with precision and carried conviction to the audiences. She has been there all the time, reaching out and touching the minds and hearts of people and not merely entertaining them.

All those who met her had positive things to say, be it a dancer, critic or scholar. She also had a circle of intellectuals as her fans and supporters, such as Pearl Buck and Ananda Coomaraswamy.

It was a time when Indian dance forms were not known to the West. India was a colony and there was not much information available about it either. It was only when the Round Table Conference was held in London and India's struggle for freedom came to the forefront that some kind of consciousness about India reached the West. Under these circumstances, La Meri managed to put together a group of students whom she trained to perform Indian dance in London on India Day. She created an interest in understanding what India had to offer and made Indians proud and happy about their culture and heritage.

It is well known that in the early part of last century, an act had been passed banning dance in temples. The performers, i.e. devadasis were looked down upon. The great pioneer Rukmini Arundale (who did not belong to the devadasi class) brought back the dance of Bharatanatyam with force, so that the art form could be appreciated again at a deeper level. She endeavoured to revitalise its pristine spirit of devotion. It is approximately at this time too that La Meri and her students performed the classical dances of India in foreign lands.

She created an interest in ethnic dance forms and organised scholarships and teacher-training programmes. She presented summer festivals in which dancers from different countries performed. The summer festivals which she held were successful because they gave many artistes an opportunity to perform as well as be exposed to larger audience, who were becoming more sophisticated and familiar with what other cultures had to offer.

Thus she was responsible for a generation of students of Indian dance, who later became well-known solo artistes and trained teachers in their own right. La Meri gave cosy theatre programmes at the studio which helped audience to appreciate Indian and other dance-forms, thereby enlarging their horizons.

La Meri said, "For me the only joy in living is to give and to give greatly, while yet there is time".

1

LOOKING THROUGH A MIRROR
A Glimpse of Personal Life

On 13 May 1898, to Lily Allan, a beautiful woman with a strong streak of Scottish stubborness and hardworking husband Russel Hughes was born Russel Meriwether Hughes or La Meri (as she was called later), in an elegant home in Louisville Kentucky.

From infancy she was used to travelling with her parents and enjoyed it. They moved to San Antonio in 1900. Her mother Lily pursued her penchant for elegant living, continued to call formally on the few ladies with card cases in French gloved hands whom she would approve of every Tuesday afternoon, arrayed in velvet tea gown, she received callers at home. Lilian, her elder sister and she, enjoyed San Antonio from the beginning. The school, horse-riding and even getting beaten by Lilian while playing marbles and jack stones were all happy events of her life. Lilian was her ideal. As a tiny tot, she copied all the things her sister did, including learning to play the violin. As a result of her determined effort, she started playing in the local symphony orchestra from the age of twelve.

Her father was the owner of the first 'gas buggy' in San Antonio and became famous for reaching 'the hair raising speed of 15 miles per hour'.

Her childhood and adolescence were packed with varied creative and energetic activities. She studied ballet from the age of twelve and enjoyed dancing different kinds of dances. She wrote poems and verses which even got published in the local papers. She was good at sports too; she rescued her sister and a few others from swimming mishaps. Her father presented her with a car when she turned thirteen and this made her all the more active and independent. Being a good student she was admitted into Columbia University but unfortunately she had to leave because of the malicious gossip of the landlady, even though her academic performance was very good.

In 1920, she saw at the 'Greenwich Village Follies', a slim girl perform a sort of Javanese dance with extraordinary supple waist turns. This fascinated her immensely and left an indelible impression. This was none other than Martha Graham. Earlier in 1912, Anna Pavlova had performed in San Antonio. La Meri remembered that she

La Meri : Performing Bharatanatyam

was not attractive to look at but when she danced, 'I could feel in the marrow of my bones a beauty of movements that the world has yet to see surpassed'. This inspired her to learn ballet and focus more on dancing. She also accepted various roles and performed them without inhibition. In May 1914 her father died. She deeply missed him.

In 1915, seeing the tall exquisite Ruth St. Denis in her glamorous potrayal of the Eastern themes in her dances, set her off on a reading spree of poetry, travel, history and philosophy of the East. In her enthusiasm she even ventured to start Oriental dance classes, which was a mixture of Moorish, Indian and Turkish styles. La Argentina,[1] the tall green-eyed fabulous Spanish dancer stirred her to learn Spanish dance and even perform in a fiesta soon after.

La Meri : with her Mother

One might think that she had a grasshopper mind but she was sincere and deeply involved with everything that she did. She learnt to play castanets in ten days and wrapped in Grandma Lucy's shawl, performed a fandango on the night of the coronation.[2] She felt at home on the stage.

> There subconscious bond of unity with an audience that can translate a performance into a lovers' dialogue. The black velvet draperies and gray floor cloth that constituted the setting for my career were my home. Here and only here, do I come to feel supremely comfortable, supremely happy—for always there is my lover facing me just across the footlights.

She joined the College of Industrial Arts in Denton, Texas, in 1916 and ran the dance department with grace. She happened to see the Diaghliev Company perform *L'Apres Midi d'un Faune, Sche'her'zade* ; etc. The emotional impact of it was so strong that she fell sick.

La Meri's Father and Mother

The First World War came and with it manifold experiences like dancing with khaki-clad stalwarts, falling in and out of love and developing a mania for patriotic activity. Soon after, she fell a victim to the Spanish flu. Even though the doctors gave up hope, her will to live pulled her through the nightmare. She believed in fighting for her goal.

> I could set my hand to whatever I liked so long as I always finished the job, recognizing that the real reward came in the joy of accomplishment; instead of standing still after completing a task, waiting for the recompensation to appear, one simply pocketed the satisfaction and without a backward glance turned to something new.

---

1. A Spanish dancer.
2. Coronation of King George VI.

This was reflected in her actions throughout her life. Dancing at the War Department and later at the Empire Theatre, which included dancing, acting and singing, made her very popular. She toured other cities and finally New York. It is from here that her life took a more definite line. She studied ballet with Tarasoff, tap dance at Chorous Equity and Spanish dance with Auriaza and Ortega.

She started job hunting in and out of mazes only to be hired to play castanets from the wings for a beautiful dancer in a vaudeville act. This acted as her fortunate stepping stone to get into the troupe of Maria Montero, who besides being the finest Spanish dancer, taught and advised her and gave her rich technical experience in dance and stage management.

She turned herself to high gear and worked hard in her hired studio and met various dance agents. She was introduced to a Spanish agent so that he could promote her Spanish dance. This was an interesting introduction to a man who later became her husband. He was an impresario who had worked for great artists like Busoni, Pavlova and Nijinsky.

The Spaniard arrived. A romantic aparition: Tall, handsome, grey haired in a distinguished way he was elegantly turned out...my eyes bulged out, I kept my mind fiercely on my work.

'Have you had any professional experience,' he enquired absently. I felt insulted 'Oh yes'. I answered crisply 'Where?' .... I blurted out 'In Mexico'—I had never been there. However I knew it is conventional for all Latin American capitals to boast National Theatres. So I added confidently, 'Theatro Nacional, in Mexico City'.

'Strange' murmured my interrogator, eyeing me, 'Theatro Nacional at Mexico City isn't quite completed yet'.

Guido Carreras

My self-confidence gave way abruptly. Unnerved, I cried, stamping my foot. To my credit be it said that I surprised myself half out of my wits. 'Well, damn it. What d'you expect a girl to say? I know you have to have had experience in order to be allowed to get any experience and how silly d'you think that is? All right, then, you want to know where my experience has been. Well, I'm the amateur pride of San Antonio, Texas and I've bummed the New York Subway Circuit—so now you know'. 'Tell me', I demanded, leaning forward belligerently, 'are you satisfied?' It was pretty rude; Mama would be horrified. But I was way beyond caring.

'Well, at least your temperament is Spanish', mused my tormentor. 'Get your clothes on and come over to my office. We will talk about a contract.' Tall, broad-shouldered, he had a sharp intellect and a monumental charm. I could not, however, ignore his charm—what female could? And our romance blossomed. We stayed in Mexico City for three months. All in all the days were magical for me. Daily, Carreras brought me little gifts, flowers, pictures, little volumes of poetry in Spanish. I struggled to keep my move secret. I wasn't sure about

Lilian, La Meri and Jo, Guido's Niece

mother. She had witnessed too many of my adolescent love affairs not to mention the springtime fever of love for Captain Johnny.

She bided her time, seemingly waiting for this, like other crushes, to evaporate in the glamour of a burgeoning career.

Mother liked Carreras personally very much. But she found ways to remind me that he was 20 years my senior; his background could hardly have been more different from my own. Nevertheless she recognized that, here at last, somebody was successfully channelling my creative talents into constructively concrete expression.

From then on, La Meri started making her own repertoire, her mother sewed the costumes and Carreras arranged for the local and foreign programmes. The first one was at the Theatro Nacional in Mexico City as fate would have it.

It also happened that she was christened 'La Meri' in Mexico City by a magazine called *Slick*. This appealed to the public and 'La Meri' she became. She tasted glamour and success and it encouraged her to study different Spanish and Latin American dances from excellent teachers. So when she went back to New York she got into the concert artiste circuit as the 'Queen of the Spanish Shawl'. Her shawl dance was spectacular and one of the most popular numbers till the end.

Her mother who was a great support and company for her, died in March 1927.

Though she was highly disturbed, she embarked on many tours and they were packed with adventures just like in a storybook. The escapades in the Caribbean were many.

I was not always as successful in dealing with the human fauna. The overly zealous piripos, compliments, to put it more kindly, of the Cuban equivalent of drugstore cowboy, annoyed me. One day when several of them followed me, I became alarmed. My studiedly dignified walk accelerated until it became an ungainly trot. With relief I reached the hotel. My tormentors followed me in. I complained to the desk clerk. To him discretion was evidently very much the better part of valor; as this comet's tail of undesirables now numbered at least a score and was growing. The clerk declined to order them from the lobby. In near panic I started up the broad staircase. Two of the crowd bounded after me.

At that moment, like the legendary U.S. Marines, my manager materialized at the top of the stairs. Some well-chosen if not very refined remarks were showered down on the men by my knight. Other members of our company, housed on the second floor, caught the rising racket of shouts and rushed out to reinforce our side. A little emboldened now, the reluctant desk clerk got around to calling police. Waiting for them to arrive, Carreras, the Russian cellist and the Italian pianist held back the mob, impaling it on red-hot points of diatribe.

In Cuba in those days peep-holes in the dressing rooms were *de riguevr.* The first job of any visiting artiste was to stop up the holes with wads of cleansing tissue or hanging clothes; or, in the holes which were near the floor, with suitcases. Shoes were no good for they had a way of walking, apparently under their own power. My dressing room in Ponce looked out onto a patio and was shuttered. I stopped all discernible holes. Still, putting on my make-up, I had a queezy sense of bold eyes taking a good look-see. Indignantly I located Carreras and demanded immediate measures. He strode out into the patio, taking care to make no noise and sure enough, a dark, crouching figure had eyes glued to the shutters of my dressing room. Silently Carreras fetched a fearful kick to the seat of the pants. And who did our peeping Tom turn out to be? None other than regular critic of the town's leading newspaper!

The love between Carreras and her grew and as far as she was concerned, she was his wife. 'I took it for granted, that when he judged the moment right, there would be a wedding. In my eyes, he could do no wrong. As for me, everything I said, did or thought was to please him, to earn a look or word of approval'.

More adventures followed. Billy[3] and she got the tropical fever.

The fever proved stubborn. Day dragged after day. I was so afraid that I wouldn't be able to dance as soon as I got out, that when the nurses, backs were turned, I sneaked into the bathroom and practised, to keep in shape. Returning from one of these sneak practice sessions, I fell on my face in a faint, bloodying my nose and loosening a couple of teeth and Carreras was there like the champion solving them all.

After going back to San Antonio, she and Lilian opened the house and enjoyed giving parties to friends while they continued to rehearse and prepare new items and costumes. In 1928, she was booked in a theatre just off Broadway. Her destiny was settled. She made her debut as a solo concert dancer at the John Golden Theatre in New York on 6 May 1928.

3. A member of her troupe.

La Meri : Performing Peacock Dance

The very air of New York at that time was a stimulus to creative work; I do not believe any other decade has produced so many creative, sometimes iconoclastic, dance artistes. Many were Denishawn trained, but World War I had engendered a rebellion against romanticism and against the courtly exactitude of ballet. In Germany Mary Wigman led the way and with the artistic expressions of shadowy Isadora Duncan spurring them on, these gallant pioneers fought for the right of the individual artiste to express himself as he elected. Doris Humphrey and Charles Weidman, Martha Graham, Agnes DeMille and a host of others were drawing about them dedicated students and giving as many performances as finances allowed to whatever public might appear.

I cannot claim to have drawn a very large audience, but friends, flowers, applause made it seem to me very glamorous and arrived artiste. The critics were divided in their opinion but not unkind and Charles Isaacson gave me a column of unqualified approval. His judgement was a benison of encouragement as I went about preparing for a South American tour which was to begin in June.

During her tour in Caracas, President Gomez invited her for a special performance in his summer palace and showed his rare collection of white peacocks, for he was very impressed by her peacock dance. This again was one of the popular items in her repertoire.

Life is always full of ups and downs. She learnt to take them in her stride.

In Marcaibo (Columbia) I shared my solo program with a democratic collection of bats and rats which scurried happily about the stage, ignoring the performance, but causing consternation among the lily-livered foreign artistes. There was an interesting extra-added attraction. It was some Saint's Day and the Governor, sitting attentively in the stage box had to call out soldiers to stop the audience from shooting off fire-crackers in the aisle. All in all I think I gave the most courageous and least artistic performance of my life. In Baranquila a group of Americans invited us to a mint julep party. Happily I do not care for mint julep. It made the matinee colourful. Bristol played the entire show without once hitting a right note. How Lilian stayed on her feet is anybody's guess.

They had more adventure, for even when all their money was stolen they managed to continue with their tour. Another lucky break she had was an opportunity to take part in 'The Vision Veracotcho'.[4]

The rest of the tour was gratifying too. On a hot afternoon in early November I was taking my usual afternoon rest after a hard morning rehearsal, when suddenly and quite inexplicably I felt an unwanted panic about Lilian. I walked the floor and cried and wrung my hands. Only the necessity of giving the evening's performance calmed me. It was years later that Lilian and I, checking on differences of time in the two hemispheres, found that at the exact time of my panic, she was in childbirth and calling for me. I never saw her twins, who did not live to see their first Christmas.

During my season in Santiago a series of earthquakes shook the southern part of Chile. We put on two shows in full for the earthquake sufferers. Already a darling of the public, this upped my popularity another notch. President-elect Herbert Hoover was on a goodwill tour

4. An annual festival.

of South America and arrived in Chile during these days. Imagine my delight when he wrote me, in longhand, commending my help in inter-American friendship. A few days later I met Mr Hoover and his beautiful wife, at a gala reception given by the American Ambassador.

My career, I felt, was going brilliantly. I had met every challenge, by dint of endless hours of joyous work, to overcome them. Love had decoyed me into putting myself so under Carrera's domination that I scarcely dared even answer when he spoke to me. Worst of all, I began to agree with his assumption that all Americans were inferior; as for God, He did not exist. When it came to my career I was as convinced as he professed to be, that I was not really an artiste at all, merely a hardworking Trilby to his omnipotent Svengali. So, while my life on the stage was glamorous in the extreme, my personal life was as controlled as a nun's.

On little river-boats we chugged up the glossy waters of the Rio Parana, Lomas de Zamorra, Cardoba, Rio Quatro, Villa Maria, Sanna Fe, Paranaa, Corrientes, Resistencia, Saenz-Pena, Posadas, Concordia, Salto, Gualelguaycho, Asuncion—I danced in them all. Now social form is rather strict in Argentina and a visiting artiste must be extremely careful of her behaviour, lest it be misunderstood. I declined the honor and suggested that the interviewer come to my hotel. The editor, feeling much put out, was scathing in his review of my debut, expressing opinion that my hula was vulgar. To our surprise the local Catholic paper took up the cudgels in my favour and declared the hula as I danced it, a model of naive charm. With each issue of each paper the war of words built up. Of course, all this fortuitous publicity reflected at the box office. We stayed quite a long while in that town.

On the night of my performance in a raw oil boom town, the classic section of my program drew only polite applause from the full house. But when I appeared in Spanish costume I was greeted with cacophonous sound, whistles, shouts, remarks not too refined in nature. I left the stage insulted and in tears. My manager left his spotlights and went out and told the public to behave itself. Words hurtled back and forth, not to mention threats and curses. The Mayor hurried backstage and demanded that Carreras apologize to the public. This he refused to do. So they took him off to spend the night in jail!

Without doubt the highlight of our river-trip was Asuncion. Not in years had an artiste visited this capital city of Paraguay. Besides being isolated, the country had been at war for so long that money was very scarce and most of the people could hardly afford to buy shoes for their feet. My arrival was a sensation. We announced one concert, but during the intermission every seat was sold for a second. After five performances we found ourselves so affluent that we decided to take time out for a hunting trip up in the Chaco.

We rented a small motor-launch and, early one June morning, set out up the river. The party consisted of our manager, myself, Cendalli and three members of our local orchestra, plus three hunting dogs. It was the dark hour before dawn when we started across the wide water that leaves Asuncion. Halfway across the dogs began to whine and move about and we discovered that our little boat, greatly overloaded, was seeping water to an alarming degree. I say alarming because those waters are alive with the small fishes which will eat the flesh right off the bones of any unfortunate living creature which falls prey to them.

This South American tour gave La Meri the first real sense of being a recognised concert dancer. She felt artistically more armed, fortified to assimilate from what lay ahead in new environments. While returning home in the boat, as the tension diffused, she danced on the gently rolling deck rediscovering the joy of dancing for its own sake, with the universe as a stage and the stars as audience.

As the tour continued, along with concerts and adventures she was also learning their local dances from good teachers. In Granada she worked with Manual Defalla to produce *Amor Brujo*. Here she learnt authentic gypsy dances from one of the best dancers, who taught her not for money but due to her keen interest. Her adventurous spirit was boosted further by the encounter with a bullfighter.

I danced a concert in Granada, which made my name known. Forthwith a young bullfighter (aged 17 and making his debut) sent a member of his *cuardrilla* to ask if I would permit him to dedicate a bull to me on the following Sunday. With what alacrity I accepted! I sat in a box. His *capa de luz* was draped across the front of it. And when he threw his hat to me in formal dedication I was, Carreras notwithstanding, in love with him, even though I had never set eyes on him (or, more's the pity, since). Just to round out the drama of the occasion, the bull caught and flung him into the air. Naturally I screamed—without realizing it. Happily sustaining only a broken rib, the *torero* rose in a fury, killing the bull with such neatness and dispatch that he was awarded ears and tail. I kept the bull's smelly old tail for years, a memento of having once played Carmen in real life.

In Sevilla I came under the tutelage of the great Otero. In the mornings I took private lessons; at night, class lessons at Otero's studio. A whitewashed house, like all the others, with a wrought iron gate. Being a bachelor establishment there are few flowers in the cool patio. To the right was the dancing room. About 20 feet square, this room is historic. The walls are covered with coloured posters of the bullfights; the floor, filthy with three generations of *taconeo*, sags and bounces when danced upon. Chaste wooden benches line the walls and a wheezy piano stands in the corner.

In Sevilla she made her tailed dress, Traje de cola by the dressmaker who made the costumes for the famous Pastora Imperio.[5] She did not waste even one moment. She went to Morocco to Fez to see the Moorish dance in its native background. The favourite dancer of the Sultan taught her many dances. Coming to Florence she took a break and settled in a home and got a studio to rehearse and enlarge her repertoire to be ready for the forthcoming programme in Vienna. Vienna, the cultural summit of Europe, was also the home of the editor of the *Neue Frie Presse*, Felix Cleve, Europe's premier authority on dance, drama and motion pictures. In Vienna,

Our money was low. For the sake of face, I was installed in a suite in the Grand Hotel, with Lilian while Carreras and Dallapiccola took the very cheapest rooms in the wilds of the top floor. For dinner, while Lilian hid in my bathroom, I would order a weiner schnitzel for one. When the waiter had gone, Lilian and I would make a meal for two out of it. Vienna had no confidence in artistry being inherent in any American. The easiest conclusion to reach was that I was a rich young eccentric, dabbling in art. Upon my first performance, Dr. Cleve and the lesser critics alike came out with fine reviews. In fact, Cleve gave me what remains to this day the finest and fairest review I have ever had. Its greatest value was that it taught me a great deal, for in it he let me see my flaws as well as the virtues of my performance.

5. A famous Spanish dancer.

In Berlin, again her performance was well appreciated for its philosophies of movement. Here she had the pleasure of becoming Mary Wigman's friend.

At the opening of the week, a big banquet was given for the performers. Pavlova and I sat opposite each other at the long narrow table. I was struck dumb, but she was serenely gracious. She told me that she knew I was a specialist in the ethnic field. 'I would like you to give your candid opinion of my Mexican dances', she said and she said it in a way that made me feel she was really anxious to have the opinion of a fellow artist.

I have often wondered why, in all the millions of words written about her, so little has been said of her insatiable interest in the ethnic dance-arts. She not only learnt, but staged the dances of Mexico. It was she, also, who discovered Shankar and played Radha opposite his Krishna. He has since told me that she often cried bitterly because she felt she was so inept in mastering the true Indian style. She also learnt and staged the dances of Japan and of Spain. Here, then, was no single-minded classicist. She saw all dances of all the world as equally beautiful, equally worthy.

In answering this bewildering request for an opinion of her *Jarabe* I was strictly on my own, for Carreras happened to be sitting some distance from me and I could not turn to him for help. I don't remember now exactly what I said to her. I remember only that I discovered I could discuss dancing objectively and intelligently that I felt perhaps for the first time, that I had ideas on the subject which were definite and my own. I remember too that it was at this banquet that the last photograph of Pavlova was made. En route from Oslo to Hamburg she was stricken with the illness that killed her.

Next stepping stone for La Meri was the Paris concert. She worked real hard for it.

We saw wonderful plays and concerts, Argentina, in her production of *El Amor Brujo* and Uday Shankar and his company, giving me my first sight of East Indian dancing. I could not know how much it would mean to my future, but I went away from that performance walking on air. What an excitingly beautiful art! What a matchless artist to communicate it!

Uday Shankar and La Meri

I took courage in my hands and introduced myself to this God-like dancer. I found him a simple and sympathetic human being. I entreated him to give me lessons. He insisted that he did not teach, but invited me to his home on the outskirts of Paris. In their airy villa I met his charming companion-artistes and we settled down on the floor, Indian style, while he explained to me a little of the vast lore of Indian dance. Finally he gave me some records and some books to study and told me that if I would make my own dance he would correct them in lieu of lessons. I haunted his

La Meri with a Maori teacher

rehearsals and performances and myself spent long happy hours creating an Indian dance. I titled it *Lasyanatana*. Twice Shankar worked with me in correcting it and eventually I had an authoritative Indian dance which remains with me to this day.

This encounter with Uday Shankar acted as a catalyst in her future.

In her personal life, marriage to Carreras was from the beginning full of ups and downs.

In June of 1931 he and I got around to marrying. As it was awkward for him to remarry in a Catholic country, he went to London while I stayed on some 10 days in Paris, putting together a modest trousseau.

After four years of anxiously awaiting this outcome I found, to my horror, that I felt qualms. I had nightmares and abrupt crying spells and the near-panic of claustrophobia. Perhaps, I told myself it was only a bride's usual jitters. Or perhaps, I tried not to tell myself, it was a deep, inner conflict between my bedrock layer of old-fashioned propriety and my new-burgeoning strength as an artiste. We were married the next day by a beaming if rather seedy looking civil clerk, in a dingy, mid-Victorian registry. The only others present were the two witnesses, Mr Lord of the American Consulate and the dancer, Maud Allen. When the knot had been tied, Carreras left to take Miss Allen home, where he spent the next several hours arranging for me to give a dance recital in her beautiful Hyde Park residence. I walked back from the Registry to the hotel alone.

We went from London direct to Italy, taking a cottage by the sea in a tiny Tuscan village called Ronchi. Happy to be back among Italians again, my husband spent most of his time among the local menfolk, while I turned to my typewriter and wrote my first full length book on dancing *Dance as an Art Form*.

A good part of their honeymoon was complicated by a long visit of her mother-in-law who took her to be a femme fatale. 'We moved in the autumn to Florence, where Carreras placed me on the faculty of the state-subventioned R. Academia dei Fidenti. Here I held classes, staged ballets and occupied myself quite happily. In some ways I found my evening classes, given gratis to working-girls, more satisfying'.

They often went to the sea to swim and sail and then played tennis, while Carreras went for trap shooting. He asked her also to join and practise for a competition. The man in the trenches wanted her to win so he made some adjustments to the speed of the clay pigeon.

> Like myself, he was over-excited. The 'bird' lumbered up with all the speed of an overfed thanksgiving turkey to a height of some four feet, whereupon it collapsed to the ground. Blasting away, I hit the top of the sandbags, bringing the poor man gasping to his feet. He had sought to help me and for his troubles had eyes, ears, nose and mouth filled with sand. 'O, Senora!' he chided me through sand-covered teeth. A miracle of self-control. Thus did I become acquainted with Averardo, who worked with us for 15 years.

In 1932, they went home to Italy and enjoyed the familiar places. She loved the country more and felt very American. She also gave her book to be published. She settled in Fidenti in a lovely villa near the beach with a beautiful studio and Averardo came to help them. The year that followed was filled with visits from friends and family, parties and receptions. She also gave dance classes and presented outdoor festivals, so much so that Vienna Dance Congress invited her to join them representing Italy.

In Vienna she enjoyed being a jury member and seeing many dance-events. The two concerts presented at the Congress were one by Great Weisenthal, one of the most inspiring dancers who moved as though the music was flowing from her lovely body; and the other was by her.

> It was my all ethnic performance and I was received with a warmth I was never to forget—how an artiste feels, with a quivering antenna of the heart, the waves which sweep across the footlights from the audience. Before the first dance was half performed, Vienna and I were in love as ideally as audience and artistes can be.

There were repeated cries for encore. Finally she came to the stage and said, 'Die program ist sehr shnell. Ich bin Kaput, Aber ich liebe dich':[6] which brought more applause and laughter. This experience aroused in her a great desire to perform more and learn more. Her next chance came when Princess San Faustino in Rome involved her as a soloist and choreographer for the presentation 'Triunfo del grano' where she was highly appreciated and was invited again to do 'quo vadis'.

London gave a cool welcome but before the first week was over she had been booked for sixteen performances including one for the India Society. London season proved to be a great success which gave her more self-confidence to dance for the joy of it.

The next boon that came her way was a contract from an Australian impresario which could fulfil her dreams of entering the enchanting realms of the Orient.

---

6. 'The programme is fast and I am tired, but I love you.'

La Meri with G.K. Seshagiri and Kalyan Sundaram

She embarked at Geneva for Australia on 5th May 1936. Mr Longden, the Australian agent was frightened to death at his temerity in bringing a solo dance concert to Australia for it had not seen any since Maud Allen's concert in 1911. Fortunately the debut on 20 June was very successful and instead of eight they ended giving twenty-two performances. She performed sixty different dances during this engagement and it delighted her to know that many people bought tickets and sat in the same seat for every performance. They toured many cities and on the fifty-seventh concert as she ran on to the stage, she heard a snap and could not move. It was a torn muscle and she had to rest for three weeks. This was a blessing in disguise for she went to Roturua in New Zealand to recuperate where the Maoris loved her. She also learnt Maori dance from Guide Bellow who was seventy years old but appearing fifty and dancing like twenty. Before she left she gave them a concert which they enjoyed and appreciated and she for one felt that she danced better than ever.

She had to make-do with records for the rest of the tour—108 concerts in five months! It was a glamorous tour and the press said clear and loud 'that she had blazed a trail'.

Coming closer to her land of dreams, they landed in Colombo and travelled to Kandy where she promptly learnt Kandian dance from Ratharana and bought herself a gorgeous costume. Later she left for Madras. 'I like Madras best.', she said, for she met many people of charm and intellect. 'My first audience was all British and the second all Indian—I was frightened to death about the Indian dances, but these people of the languorous East reassured me by shouting with joy and demanding an encore after each presentation.' The Madras (Chennai) audience is still known for its deep appreciation of dance.

It was Mr G.K. Seshagiri, the regisseur of the Indian Renaissance Theatre who gave her the open sesame to the rich lore of Bharatanatyam. He invited her to a recital by the two foremost Bharatanatyam exponents Varalakshmi and Bhanumathi.[7]

---

7. La Meri had the unique opportunity of giving a concert along with Bhanumathi and Varalakshmi in Madras. Bhanumathi belonged to a traditional devadasi family and studied Bharatanatyam under Guru Papanasam Vadivelu Pillai who belonged to Meenakshi Sundaram Pillai's school.

   Bhanumathi continued performing till 1954. She was awarded many titles and in 1978 received the Sangeet Natak Akademi award for her distinguished services in promoting Bharatanatyam.

'Perfectly trained in an incredibly complicated technique, they were to borrow from Degas' she described. Mr Seshagiri made it possible for her to study Bharatanatyam from their teacher—Guru Papanasam Vadivelu Pillai.

La Meri with Varalakshmi and Bhanumathi

Guru Vadivelu in the beginning was skeptical and somewhat sarcastic. However, he too learned something during that same first lesson, namely that I had the capacity to work for hours at a stretch without resting and, whereas his other pupils would burst into tears and rush from the room, that I could take any amount of correction.

Back in the hotel after lunch and two hours of rest, she practised the steps she had learnt in that morning for three hours. By the third lesson Guru remarked that she could learn in a month what other students took one year to master and that with six months of training he would make her the best dancer in India. At the end of the eighth lesson he cut it down to three months.

Guru Papanasam Vadivelu Pillai

I think the reason we got on rapidly was that I had as much admiration for him as a teacher as he had for me as a pupil. It was stimulating to me too that other teachers, poets, musicians and indeed all the colony of dance-lovers dropped in at all my lessons. I was, it seemed, the newest and most intriguing Bharatanatyam phenomenon.

Her will to learn and achieve things was very strong as one sees from her Indian experience.

When she was at Bangalore giving a concert, a young man came to meet her. He spoke knowledgeably on dance in fluent English and expressed his desire to join her troupe. 'From all the letters of auditions I had been given, the youngster stood out. He impressed me most, even if he did perform a dance of India to the music of Ravel's *Bolero*. He was so anxious to join us that, after a talk with his very charming family, we agreed to take him along.' This was Bassano Ram Gopal who became an inspiring exponent of Indian dances outside India and became very popular in U.K. He also helped La Meri in understanding the Indian dances better and to perform and appreciate it.

She returned to Madras and continued her study by learning *abhinaya* from Srimati Gauri Ammal. Her lesson from the two gurus took all day. She also had endless discussions with many and gathered invaluable knowledge of the much beloved art.

The finale of her Madras stay was a concert presented by Mr Seshagiri.

La Meri and Ram Gopal

The performance itself was in two parts. The first half was given over to contrasting types of western dance, performed by me. The second was dedicated to Bharatanatyam items, done by Vijayalakshmi and Bhanumathi, assisted—and I think about it to this day with pride—by me. In this half I did one solo. After an applauded sequence of mine, Guru said 'once more'. I danced the dance sequence three times—whether because of the audience or to give Vadivelu a chance to show off his English, I cannot be sure. Half of Madras was down at the station to see us off after my last concert there. Dancers, poets, musicians, critics—they presented us with flower garlands and nice speeches, touching us greatly with their gentle kindness.

This experience was rich and meaningful for her. It helped her to set up Bharatanatyam courses and increase her ability to grasp other Oriental dances. For the first time she realised how the hands can speak and later she wrote a book on the hand gestures used in Indian classical dances.

She toured Hyderabad, Bombay, Nagpur and relished the various aspects of the audiences. She narrates that the train travel in India was not easy and that the 'bearer' phenomenon was very quaint in the 1930s. The 'bearer' had to take the luggage and the bedding and occupy the compartment hours ahead of time and after arranging everything in order, brought a huge chunk of ice and left them, to travel in a third class compartment.

La Meri with Srimati Gauri Ammal

In Calcutta she had the ingenuity to assemble and rehearse with an Indian orchestra, to record the dances she had learnt in Madras, as well as some numbers of Ram Gopal. No time was wasted in achieving her goal; she also managed to see programmes of the local artistes and gave interviews and talks. She then came to New Delhi. Her first impression of this city was 'of an exposition, but one not yet opened, the avenues were deserted; there were no cattle, no dogs, no people, in fact no signs of life but for occasional speeding automobiles.' (Alas ! those days are now mere illusions.) They had successful concerts at Lahore and later visited the Golden Temple at Amritsar which she liked the most.

In Lucknow she went to learn Kathak under Sri Ram Dutt Misra.[8]

After my travail with the Spanish flamenco, I did not find Kathak too difficult since it is based largely on rhythmic floor contacts. The Indians who came to watch my lessons were amazed at my ability in the footwork, which, to them, is the most difficult part of the dance.

8. Sometimes she refers to him in Lahore as well.

It would seem almost as if their arms and hands can be trusted to move quite by themselves, whereas I would have to go home and struggle for hours to make mine move decently at all.

La Meri with Sri Ram Dutt Misra

With seven hours of lessons and rehearsals every day, she managed to give a concert in Delhi on her return from Lucknow. She reflects that the months spent in India were so profound that it had taken her nearly twenty years to fully savour it. Perhaps unwittingly, 'I found in the golden dust landscape, in the serenity of the temples, in the dark, deep eyes of simple people, a clearer sense of values and a philosophy for loving. I know that it was in India I reached a point at which my work became predominantly important to me, a point at which I began to feel that I was important to my work. I began to find new strength within myself, fresh faith in my own capabilities. The little puppet Trilby began to dissolve.'

During this period, India's exposure to Western art was only through movies except for few earlier visits of Pavlova and Denishawn to the four metros. At the beginning of their tour, writers had observed that 'West must come to the East to learn true artistry' but by the end of the season they had seen and acknowledged the beauty, especially seeing her *Madonna*, a dance of a different religion, performed to strange music and depicting a strange painting.

I felt that on a smaller scale we did for western art what Shankar did for Indian art in the West. Great nationalists, the Indians, openly loved my renderings of their dances. The mystics declared me a reincarnation of an *apsara*, while the more practical-minded said my coming was a milestone in Indian art.

The next stop was Rangoon and she loved it from the beginning. Her search for a dance teacher led her to a suburban house where the legendary dancer U.P.O. Sein lived. It was very fortuitous that just as she got there Sein's two big black Cadillas pulled up and his company alighted. Though he danced for them and showed his costumes, he told them that he was an artiste and not a teacher. She invited him to her concert and to her great surprise he came backstage after her performance and commanded that she should come to his house next morning to learn Burmese dances. Sixty year old and as agile as a boy of twelve with raven black hair falling nearly to his knees, he started a rigorous schedule of four hour classes. As he was insistent on her performing the Burmese dance for the second concert, she got the costume and record and worked out the steps. On the day of the programme, the rehearsal was memorable.

La Meri as Madonna

He came and for two hours I skittered about the stage, nearly weeping with nervousness for never did he do the dance twice in the same way, never did he finish with the record; never did I find out what rhythm he kept, if any. So much work to so little purpose.

La Meri : Taking Lessons from U.P.O. Sein in Burma

Public and critics were very pleased with her Pwe debut. She worked on it later and it became one of her best pieces. She says, 'But the time I spent learning Pwe with U.P.O. Sein I could have spent in learning three with Vadivelu.'

Her journey continued with its ups and downs and surprises from Rangoon to Kuala Lumpur, to Singapore and finally to Java. During this six day voyage she continued with her rehearsals and lessons with Ram Gopal. It was during the voyage that she could analyse the well of loneliness in which she lived.

Perhaps this inner life might have died of malnutrition except for the stream of mail from Lil. I looked forward hungrily to the packets of letters, papers and boxes that awaited me at scheduled stops along the way. I read her long, chatty letters over dozens of times and wrote her assiduously from trains, boats and backstage. All the clothes in my limited personal wardrobe were things that she had grown tired of, or had picked up for me in her shopping jaunts. Because she sent them to me they had for me a very special glamour of their own. To her I was forever her little sister, a human being; she regarded my artistic successes with gratification not unmixed with surprise. And Dave,[9] God bless him, loved me dearly, but believed in his heart that his wife could dance better.

How often was I to lock myself in my state room to weep alone, knowing that, at least when the curtain went up, I wouldn't be lonely.

La Meri and Ram Gopal Performing a Mexican Dance

The Batavia Theatre was in the zoo. One of the baby elephants became so attached to Ram Gopal that it followed him around. It is here that he made his debut as a Mexican dancer. Besides giving performances in other cities they both organised several conferences on Indian dance on this tour. She also learnt the teaching methods of Indonesian dances as she was invited by the Princes of Solo and Djokaja to learn from their classes at the palace. Besides, she attended many performances. She says that night after night they performed the same Rama epic dramas that had been enacted for centuries and always to a full house. There was a sense of enchantment created by the stately stylised movements of the actors and the heady hypnotic music along with the aroma of spicy cigarettes.

9. Lilian's husband.

La Meri and Ram Gopal Performing an Indonesian Dance

In the Philippines they had problems as authorities insisted that Ram Gopal and Rajoo (tabla-player) had to go to detention, the goods were not released, their programme was not announced. The officials had to be bribed to get the papers rectified and therefore they had to stay and give concerts so that they could buy tickets to sail for China. In spite of all this, she managed to learn Filipino dances from Mme Reyes Tolentino.

Their stay in Hong Kong was perfect, with performances in a good theatre to full houses but they left, just in time before the bombs dropped on the city.

She sailed into Japan and spent about three months in a rented house in Tokyo. Here they rehearsed, got a seamstress to mend and make new costumes and went to many theatre shows. She started her lessons in Japanese dancing from Mme Kodera, dancer and teacher of a great repute. Here also they were impressed by the speed of her learning. The teaching system was for the teacher to do the dance over and over again until the pupil grasped it gradually.

As Mme Kodera repeated the dance several times I would write down the number and form of the steps. I drew on the terminology of Hindu, Spanish and ballet dancing and anyone who chanced to look over the notes would have been able to take them only for psychotic images of a mental patient. However, checking and properly correcting them, I would spend several hours, between lessons, in fitting the music and steps together and the hardest work was done. The next lesson could be spent on gestures and next on polishing the whole. Thus I learnt six Japanese classical dances in five weeks.

La Meri was asked to give an illustrated lecture on the Indian origins of Japanese dance. She made great preparations for this along with an exhibition of costume and it went off well. However, the war reared its head. So they had to cancel other plans and leave for the U.S. They shipped Rajoo back to India but Ram Gopal decided to stay back in Japan and wait for a chance to go to the U.S. to go on with his career.

They sailed away from Japan with a heavy heart. To her surprise, she heard that the popular gossip had marked her as the spy Mata Hari !

Getting closer to home, sailing in the luxury boat, she was enjoying it. At Honolulu they were met by Bable, their local agent. She immediately got in touch with the Hula teacher the very hour she arrived. She started taking lessons every day during her stay. Her sister Lilian had the privilege of working with the great Ana Hilla, the last representative of the old, classic style of technique and La Meri was determined to enrich her repertoire. One enchanted evening against the sensuous background of the tropical garden, they had the pleasure of seeing Winona Love, the greatest Hawii *Olapa* give a special programme. Dressed in black satin *Holoku* and many fragrant white *leis*, she danced like a living poem.

With scarcely any movement of feet or hips, her flowing hands flowered on the white veins of her arms while her lovely face as enraptured as that of a dreaming child, lifted to express all the naive joy of a tropical civilization now lost in the mists of long gone yesterdays.

Lilian and La Meri

They unfortunately lost Mr Longden,[10] their efficient manager who went back to Europe. Her personal unhappiness was disturbing her work and Dave, her brother-in-law helped her to see things better.

At the best, the human soul is isolated in loneliness in its shadowy journey through life, even reaching out through a confusion of speeches for a companionship of sympathy and understanding. How rarely is it found! Dave's calm, little spoken philosophy of day-to-day living, honest, clear, courageous, was a wonderfully strengthening thing to know.

She and her sister were very close and wrote frequently long letters to each other and exchanged Christmas gifts and Lilian was very generous with her gifts. She wrote about her plans, daily activities, problems at home with Jo Carreras, the niece of her husband, feminine interest in hats, sewing, clothes, make-up, etc. She discussed funny incidents and gossips about various common friends and even other dancers.

When she was young, she even wrote about her different boyfriends. Jess, a very good dancer once asked her to teach but her mother had a complex about Jess. La Meri then wrote to Lilian, 'I have to teach, there is a demand for it.... I do love to have the money'. Much later she found her strength was in teaching. They sent each other Christmas gifts and Lilian was very generous and thoughtful with her gifts.

Lilian and Dave

In August 1942, Guy and she went apartment hunting.

Jo was disappointed because there was no studio for her to practise. I had a show-down talk with Guy. If Jo wants to live with us she can pay board; if she wants to study with me, she can pay for her lessons. She is an extremely disagreeable young lady and I will not be beholden to her any longer. I have put up with it at least two years longer than I should have.

And while later she writes, 'Jo, as a matter of fact I watch her sometimes and it is strange that she really is a pretty good little peasant girl.... A good kid, but she suffers with misplaced

10. Mr. Longden was her tour manager, he was from Australia.

La Meri with her Dogs

priorities'. This swing in her relationship with Jo continued but she loved her and dedicated her book on Spanish dancing to her.

La Meri was sensitive about students and arranged scholarships for many who could not afford the tuition fee. She went to Mandel's dance recital once and she felt strongly about the casual way Mandel was treated.

Neither Miss Ruth nor any of her stooges were there... and I was mad. If she does not approve of the kid artistically or racially, then she should not have her in her studio. If she has any kind of artistic or personal sympathy then she should be present and not take the poor child's hard earned dollars as rent. I think it is disgraceful. I appreciate Mandel's idealism founded only on an aspirational instinct, without reason, that I only wish I had the time to build her a couple of dances. She is not vulgar enough for nightclub and of course you know what the concert field is for whites, let alone negroes. She had reserved the whole front row for critics and only the one from the negro newspaper came.

It reveals the kind of atmosphere one had to work in if you were not 'in'.

At the church of inner light I gave a lecture on the divine origin of the Hindu dance. I still am hearing how our performance was the only one that had public down there gave an ovation to and the only one to give encores, etc. I have an idea that we may eventually reach the people in spite of the press and I would be glad. I think the American press is the root of about 90% of our troubles.

In February 1942, she wrote, 'I am busy, I work steadily from 11 to 9 p.m. eating my supper while I teach. Speaking of servants, Guy may buy-in half ownership of *Dance* magazine, such work would take him to New York everyday and I shall be faced with the servant problem... dammit all'. It is obvious that Guy helped a lot with housework and he did the cooking and that too really well.

La Meri wrote about her tour plans to different parts of the world and the costumes that she was preparing for them. Whenever she had financial problem she asked Lilian for help. She very frankly discussed other personalities with her, e.g. Maud Allen and Ruth St. Denis were rivals but they were both her friends. She wrote even silly things like, 'How to do the eyes with false eye lashes'. Or to share the joy of her dog Pallino who travelled with her everywhere. She wrote, 'At the moment he is chewing up my deck pad, I have asked him to chew up my past, but he seems more interested in my future'. When Pallino died, she wrote, 'I miss Pallino a lot on nice days, when

I am home and could go walking. I never saw any sense in country walking without a dog.' She loved dogs and she always had one or two at home.

La Meri was also proud of her work. For she wrote:

In the reunion the girls performed solos choreographed by themselves. But it was a satisfaction to have several people say, that they showed up far better in the ballet...that is just because of my own astute choreography. Walter Terry called to say that my Bolero was the best he has seen. However as Guy has observed, he seems to keep that opinion a secret between him and me.

She learnt to drive and she was so thrilled about it for she could drive around with her troupe. 'I am so happy, now that I can drive', she wrote with pride.

At the Waldorf grand ballroom Natya Company performed representing India. We felt very proud to be representing India at such a gathering of 1,500 important personalities, where we danced a choreographic arrangement of *The Farmer from Madras*. Many people including Indians took us for Indians. The programme came first and the speeches afterwards and as a political meeting it was a wonderful study of diplomatic insincerity. Every Eastern speaker hinted or spoke of India's freedom from Britain. Bajpai (Indian Ambassador to US) sent a message which sounded a somewhat false note in the proceedings and must make the Indians against him, as his was definitely the only pro-English voice. Thank goodness I was sitting in a box with pro-Indians so I could clap as loud in the places I felt like. The morning paper quoted only important parts of the speeches; 1,500 people get together to express their opinions on Indian freedom and the press makes it sound like a social party.

As evident from the above mentioned quote, La Meri, had a genuine soft corner for India and the freedom struggle. She also wrote, 'On May 16th we met Rohit in a shop, he tells me that India League is arranging for Gandhi to speak direct to U.S.A. You all must try not to miss it'.

La Meri was very good with needlework. She was very fond of hats and in all her travels she wore hats. She wrote to Lilian, 'In the last *Companion* there is a snooty hat shown in the colour photos worn both as a hood (snood) and pulled up like a Miranda hat, she looks like a max hat and not too hard to make'. Later she wrote about the Afghan rug that she was knitting and the collots from *Vogue* that she was making for spring. She liked to live well and was house proud too. Inspite of her busy schedules she gave lovely parties at her Italian home. She wrote that her Sunday party was a success:

I cut some flowers... Dogwood and Lilac and some branches of yellow and white flowers and arranged them. It was warm enough to have all the doors and windows open. I fixed the table with white linen cloth with blue Florentine mats and over it a red and blue vase filled with white dogwood in the centre and two blue candles in silver candlesticks. All the pick-up eats were in the glass and china dishes, your spoons graced the occasion. In front of the fireplace we put the tea table and on top of it was a cask of sherry, needless to say very few people took tea. Guy and Averardo made nearly 500 dozellini and served them piping hot. They also made a gold cake which disappeared instantly. Then we had candies, olives and nuts. Jo, Mera and Marion wore their Spanish dresses and served. Mr Hassa mentioned being interested in archery and so he and some others went out on the lawn with the bows and arrows and target. I think the local ladies were pretty much swamped but I do think they enjoyed it in their own way.... It will give them something to talk about for weeks.

On 21 July 1942, she gave lectures and held classes at the Jacobs Pillow. She wrote, 'My system is to teach the good ones first and forget about the dopers. I hear everywhere the kids like my teaching, how easy I make it. The *Life* magazine wanted to know about my methodology.' Unfortunately in Ted Shawn's book nothing is mentioned about La Meri except that she taught there. She was not even given the credits for doing the Hindu dance sessions.

La Meri felt happy that her full length ethnic dance programmes were successful in New York. On the way to Mexico they stopped at their old home-town in San Antonio and she wanted desperately to 'show them' that she was professional and a successful one and so naturally it broke her heart when the house was half empty and even her old friends seemed unaware of the change in her. The deep sense of disappointment did not stop her from remembering her childhood days. She went to place flowers on the graves of her parents and had a silent communion with them. The post-concert reception was different, very warm and heartening, though she realised like all her old friends that she had also grown older. 'Here, I must shut it out of my mind, think about something else.'

She started her second round of the world tour with Mexico. 'Once more it all seemed very exciting, full of potentialities.' But her beloved Mexico had changed. When they arrived there, the customs gave them lot of troubles. In spite of bribing at different levels it was found to be a harassing manoeuvre to get their costume trunks out of their clutches. They continued with the smaller towns, finally landing at Mexico City which was as lovely as she remembered it, with its broad white *avenidas*, emerald-green plazas, calm and inviting. But the people had changed. Even during the performance, the vandals were slashing the seats with a knife. They sailed again to Lima where they performed a special concert for the Japanese Ambassador. They loved her programme. They then went to Chile where she had a strange experience. There the concert was given at Billas Arts Halls.

I was in the midst of dancing Goyescas where there was an untoward clatter from the direction of hitherto attentive audience; glancing up I saw students tumbling from their perch. I saw the earth tremor; I maintained the dance and the students calmly clambered back and the audience concentrated on observing us, quite unmoved by the hiccough by nature.

In Buenos Aires she had made no impressions the previous year. She was therefore expecting an echo of their former coolness.

One critic recalling his earlier doubts of 1928 season, wrote that having seen both Argentina and La Meri in their formative years, Buenos Aires had failed to discern the genius of either. My reaction was that if he bracketed me with Argentina, he could say anything else about me that he pleased.

They plunged next into the Columbia concert tours, which opened at St. James Theatre in New York. The friendly season's were replaced by endless one-night stands.

Lilian and Carreras's niece Juana joined her on this tour. They travelled in a chauffeured Cadillac which pulled a trailer carrying the luggage.

Uncle Ben

I cannot remember what cities we played for the trip fused into a frenzied fantasy of arrivals, shows, departures. I contracted a virus and only too often danced with a temperature of 104°F. Most of all I remember Louisville because Uncle Ben came to see my dance. He created a scandal by insisting on entering the theatre even when the programme was sold out. Unable to get rid of him, the distracted management sent a message back to me. 'God bless Uncle Ben for coming'. I cried, 'send him backstage' at once, So Uncle Ben saw the concert from a comfortable chair in the wings.' They both were attached to each other, though Uncle Ben was a difficult person to please.

In the letters she wrote during her travels one gets an insight into the deep love La Meri had for her husband Guido Carreras, who was also her manager.

> My heart is drunk for the sound of your voice.
> My eyes are blind (fluid) for your smile,
> Yet somehow my fingers can feel your hair,
> and touch your cheek a while.
> Perhaps it's because lest I die
> when we meet my heart won't realize
> till remembering finger touch your lids and open my blind eyes.

She wrote about everything to him and some of it shows her as lacking self-confidence but forthright. Once writing from the ship, she prayed,

Argentinita

Standing there on the top deck in the soft darkness all by myself, you seemed to lean right out from the shore and touch me. I half expected to turn and see you standing behind me. Leaving you there I was so afraid and I prayed fervently that the disaster I feared would happen and that you would be soon in San Antonio with me. I think I have found God again dear, because I have not been afraid again.

She adored him and missed him very much.

She became very dependent on him and this is what later made her a rebel. For earlier, she wrote to him, 'Oh, my dear it was good of God to give me the wonderful strength of your love when I needed it most. Just when I lost my mother, I was determined to become perfect for you so that you will never be sorry for you took me for yourself. I promise never to cry for anger again.'

La Meri as Mother Goddess

Carreras was a great guy. His family were great castanet makers so he knew that art too. When she had a flu he even vacuum-cleaned her room and took care of the daily chores. He was an excellent cook and he did all the cooking for parties. He and Averardo repaired the studio with all the carpentry and electrical work. He was well versed in many things. Besides being an excellent manager, he gave speeches with great success on dance. On her birthday, he decorated the room with flowers and got things under control in the kitchen. In one of her letters she says that one of the outstanding successes was Guy's characterisation of a bartender and he had written the part himself. He even acted as the ghost in one of her productions.

He was an adventurous manager and when it came to handling eveteasers or corrupt customs officials, he did very well. He had many admirable qualities. Perhaps the age difference between them and the natural growing up of the confident artiste in La Meri made them part. He wanted to be very much a part of her life but once he was sure that she did not want him, he left her in peace and never bothered her again.

The tours continued though I danced in an ominous passion of speed. My heart beat out a dirge in counter-time, the dirge of dying love. Since Australia I had been well aware that my husband was possessed of a wandering eye. Frightened and alone, I had no idea how to cope with such a state of things. More and more I retired into myself, in my confusion becoming sickeningly servile to his every whim. In even proportion I became the brilliant stage personality and the deadly social bore. My dancing began to suffer. Up to now I had danced always in the sun, out of pure joy of living. How that amazing instrument of the body reacts to the working of the mind! Muscles and sinews, schooled for years to strict discipline can be influenced by the dark moods of the mind, becoming utterly unreliable. And so it was with me.

Once when she had sprained her ankle, Carreras left her without leaving any message and came back after three weeks and without any guilt patted her shoulder, smiled and asked, 'Are you well enough to dance again?' That was all, never offered any explanation or apology. But, far down under the long habit of obedience and submission, pride stirred and self-respect, flexing they would not sleep again. Always they whispered, now the artist and woman became one, if one dies, the other cannot live.

La Meri's professional life continued to thrive. In Montevideo, Indo Bravo, a strikingly handsome woman from Madrid who was the critic of an important daily, met her and asked for the little red comb from her gypsy costume. She said, 'You see, I already wear two others, this one is from Argentina and this one from Pastora. So now you will join them. I have seen many Spanish dancers, and I shall see many more. Yet it is long that I have worn only two combs and I think it will now be long ere I wear four.' This made her feel proud and happy. However, there continued to be a clash between her professional and personal life. 'I knew now beyond all doubt, my ultimate choice would be between having a career and having myself. Which, I would have to wait a little to make sure.'

At this time the Second World War broke out. They sailed to New York. Her heart felt as empty and full of melancholy as a theatre after the show is over.

Four months later, after she had given a lecture on Indian dance and costume at the Museum of Costume Arts, a tall beautiful woman burst into her dressing room. 'My dear' she cried, 'I will not take no for an answer, I simply will not, you must open a school. Together we will open a centre for the study of Eastern arts: dance, painting, sculpture, philosophy. America is hungry for this. And only you can give it.' This was like pronouncement of a prophesy. She demanded 'Do you realize the font of knowledge you can bring to your country? The generations of youth you can feed with the knowledge of the savant and the fire of the artist? All I want is to sit at your feet and, at long last, learn the true technique of the Eastern dance.' She paused for breath. 'By the way, I am Ruth St. Denis', she said absently. Thus began a very meaningful and fruitful relationship. Though La Meri did not want to teach, for various reasons she could not forego this offer. So by midday they moved into the studio below Ruth's and opened the School of Natya. Her first pupil was the nationally well-known Jack Cole who was charming and hardworking. Many interested students could not pay for the classes, so she cut the fee down and even offered scholarships to talented and sincere students.

The device which really floated the school (and us) financially was a thing called "reunions". Weekly, on Tuesday evening, for an admission fee of seventy-five cents Ms. Ruth or I would give demonstration lectures and as our pupils began to make progress, full dance programme.

They did a very interesting programme together at the Koumanam Auditorium in New York. Ruth St. Denis explained in her opening speech, 'La Meri will do these dances as they have been done for centuries in the land of their origin. Then I will do them as I darn well please.' Ruth was absolutely wonderful to work with.

Though I felt she loved me and wanted me to succeed, there was nevertheless that sense of competition beween us which makes one work to give the very best performance possible. Let me forever record from my experience, she is a staunch and unwavering friend, that kind of very present help in time of trouble who never fails to find the answers to calm an overwrought soul in the travail of artistic creation. Apart from her immortal personal artistry, it was my happy experience to find her a tremendous woman.

Columbia University, through the intervention of Marguerite Block, the curator of the Bush Oriental Collection, asked her to complete her half written book on India's gesture-language. With determination she moved into a hotel writing ten hours a day, finished the manuscript in five days and took it to the University. The 200 illustrations were duly made from photographs. The well-known Indian scholar, Dr Ananda K. Coomaraswamy after looking at the text agreed to write the foreword. She was also invited to a presentation banquet at the University–'A proud moment for me, this University, which had cast me out years earlier.' Her good friend and dance critic Walter Terry, knowing the past history winked at her over the rim of his wineglass and shared the gentle irony as well as the happiness of the situation.

During this time she struck a beautiful friendship with the famous Spanish dancer, Argentinita[11] Lopez. Argentinita was a great human being, devoted scholar and dedicated

11. Argentinita Lopez was another Spanish dancer who became a good friend of La Meri.

to art, came to Spanish reunion and from then on dropped in often and took a hand in teaching the awestruck Natya students *Coplas* of the Sevillanas, or the *Jota*.

By now the Natya dancers were improving and were frequently giving performances and full Indian ballets composed by La Meri. These girls were young, pretty and talented and nearly all of them earned national and international acclaim.

By now Carreras was fed up of this life at the studio in New York and declared this would be the end of her as an artist. But in those hardship days, this was a haven and a fruitful one at that, though she literally worked her bones out. They moved to Mountclair in New Jersey and three days a week she would come New York at 8 a.m. and leave at 11 p.m. after teaching. In spite of all this, their financial situation was very poor. Fortunately a firm cash offer (though heartbreakingly low) for their San Antonio home was made. Lilian agreed to sell, so La Meri managed to continue her dance. The Natya dancers were very much in demand not so much for paid performances as for educational institutions. 'Artistically we were a rousing success but financially an abysmal failure.' Lilian was a great moral support; she even helped her in making costumes.

She was delighted when Ted Shawn, founder and director of Jacob's Pillow, invited the Natya dancers up for Hindu week. She also taught Spanish dance and enjoyed being with Encarna, Pilar and Federico Ray.

That August, Carreras had gotten us a season at the Hunterton Hills Playhouse in N.J. Here for five weeks we put on weekly performances spending our days in lessons and swimming in the pool. Carreras even made meal times salubrious.

I was starving for something - anything - that was my own. I went to New York to hunt for studio and succeeded in finding one. Carreras and Averado went to work to build platforms for our eventual public and lay lines for guest speakers. What a man for public relations! Suddenly we discovered we were making money and our honoured guests included Pearl Buck, Lui Yutang, Krishnalal Shridharani, Argentinita, Ruth St. Denis, Ted Shawn, Katchadourian, Felex Cleve, Margurite Block. One memorable day was spent with Ananda K. Coomaraswamy when he came down from Boston to give a lecture at the Waldorf. At the end of the lecture I was to do a dance. With Dr. Coomoraswamy to judge me, I was suffocatingly determined to dance well. To my horror I discovered the 'stage' on which I danced was constructed of a number of collapsible tables, lashed together with utmost indifference. In the evening of that same day Dr. Coomaraswamy and I did a dual broadcast and it heartened me to feel that, in the eyes of an undisputed cognoscenta of my art, I had succeeded.

La Meri with Katchadourian, Krishnalal Shridharani and A.K. Coomaraswamy

To cope with the demands of the Natya students for deeper

knowledge of the cultural background, she started summer course of Master classes. She felt most encouraged when Carlo Goya and Ruth Anderson from the Iberian Institute attended the Spanish session.

Ruth St. Denis, however, soon moved to California and left her costumes to La Meri. They took over the lease of her studio and once again Carreras and Averardo started working on it. In 1944, while talking to ballet authority Anatole Chujoy she conceived the idea for doing *Swan Lake* using Indian techniques and Chujoy enthusiastically helped her in showing the classical Petipa's choreography. It was also fortuitous that Lilian came to live in the pent house of their building.

We presented *Swan Lake* in February and it was not only a success d' estime but a respectable practical success as well. The critics gave us glowing reviews and many of the classical 'Swan Queens' amongst them Alexandra Danilova, from whom I still treasure a letter complimenting our presentation, came to view this iconoclastic version of their ballet.

This promoted them from a school to a professional theatre category. But the tension of heavy work schedule and burdened heart led to in fits of temper, often winding up in hysterical weeping, which one day lead into an argument, where Carreras said, 'You are pulling farther and farther away from me. You should remember by now, with me it is all or nothing'. 'Then let's by all means make it nothing', she said. In an unposted letter she wrote out the trauma she was having in her marital life.

Oh my lousy pussyfooting. All this romantic hoopla about closing doors gently. I have not been nice to you. Hence trying to delude myself and now I am slamming door all over the place. I don't care if you have ten girls. That is not what has made me so furious. I am sick with disgust at the sudden realization of what an abject fool I have been. It is not that you 'hurt' me; it is that you destroyed completely my self-respect and left me a snivelling mess.

Perhaps you did not notice, for you are so occupied with feeling sorry for yourself, that you have no understanding left now for anyone else in the world.

All these lost years I have let myself be made a convenience. Sit and wait, do nothing just wait until you needed a shoulder to cry on and there I was, ready willing and able. It is disgusting. I am not even human any more.

So now I run away, like the coward I am to try and figure out what it is, I hate you, or New York, or dancing and what the hell I am going to do with myself. For convenience sake, I should have died twelve years ago.

May be I will salvage something after all. I feel better already. I made the grade once (briefly), so I imagine I can make it again.

(Years later in 1968 she scribbled on this note 'God is kind, I just had a good laugh over this'.)

Mr Carreras obviously could not believe I meant this declaration of independence. In an age and a capital of super-salesmanship, I was without one iota of the talent to sell. He could not begin to understand why I should exchange my protected life for one of total uncertainty. His very failure to understand made him furious in turn and he kept harping on the idea that I must be in love with another man. Indignantly he went back to the Englewood house, to wait for me to follow. Day succeeded day and I stayed on in the studio terribly frightened of the future, but as determined as some small wood animal at bay. Performances at the theatre were going on as usual and Mr Carreras was always in evidence, making himself charming to the public during the intermissions. I did not want him there. For the first time in thirteen years, he gave me the compliments for which I had so long felt starved.

There was a strong bond of love and decency on both their sides but the differences between them had increased and both did not want to bend their egos to make the needed reconciliation.

All my work doubled and to keep my head above water, was conducted against the background music of his dark importunities. Worn down by his persistence and the overwork, I caught every vagrant virus and only too often I conducted rehearsals from an easy chair where I sat bundled to the eyes in blankets, or sewing costumes while in bed with high fever. Like Sir Galahad, my strength was the strength of ten because my heart was pure. There were evenings when the work was over, the last dancer gone from the studio, that, in the quiet loneliness of the big front room, I knew a great exaltation in this new spiritual freedom of mine.

Out of the travail of my love that had died and of the struggle for existence, there grew a new, clean creativity. It had cost me so much to buy my soul's freedom and it was yet to be proven if I could stand alone and gain a modicum of recognition for my own work. As a woman I was caught in a strange half-world, without home. But as an artiste I was happier than I had ever been. I closed the year with a production of *Alborada del Gracioso*, an abstract work built on Spanish techniques which expressed all new found creative joy, all womanly seeking for a new love. I have said before that every artiste bares his inmost soul in his works. Perhaps Mr Carreras understood me more deeply than I had known, for after he saw the *Alborada* he ceased his importunities and came no more to the studio. Presently I heard that he had gone back to Italy to live in Camplecciana. I never saw him again and he died there in 1957.

As the Natya School developed and grew, many of the best dancers left for regular employment. This did not deter her from her work. As a matter of fact she says, 'I have never, never wanted to tie my dancers to me to the detriment of their own careers, so I wished them all the luck in the world and went back to my own work'.

La Meri then worked feverishly on her 'spoken and dance production'[12] of Tagore's *Chithra* and then on *Scheherzade*. She literally crawled out of her bed with high fever and danced on the opening night. Thus bravely she battled on.

She kept adjusting to the needs of the time. When stage group shows were not possible, she resorted to solo performances of her new works–gesture songs (based on Padam's *Abhinaya* techniques). Arthur Miller got her out of town shows and with the old Ford station wagon she ploughed through sleet and snow to Chicago, Carolina, etc., with her troupe.

The Ethnologic Dance Center was a big economic drain in spite of Lilian contributing towards it. Therefore she offered scholarships and collected a talented group and started The Exotic Ballet Company.

These art hungry and egoistic children blind to the fact that I was already overworked to die of it, demanded lessons in the theories of ethnic dance. Did I refuse? Not I? I have not that

12. Exact words used by her.

kind of common sense. I was so delighted that they wanted to learn, that I added background lectures to my already overcrowded schedule. That year we presented *Bach Bharata Suite*. This was an abstract work using Hindu techniques for the interpretation of certain Bach compositions. They were all very skeptical about the outcome of it.

She humorously narrates about the press preview.

I entrusted the mixing of the cocktails to my ex-G.I.-students. By the time the curtains went up, press and public alike were feeling no pain. On the stage we dancers, conscious of the seriousness of the occasion waited nervously garbed in austere black and gold. Bach Chorali commenced—the curtains parted—and I'll declare the martinis wreathed the stage. Such deafening applause I have seldom heard, nor such enthusiastic bravos. But Mr Terry assures me that he came back the next time, just to assure himself that he had seen what he saw, through the alcoholic haze. For my next press preview, I served tea.

After two arduous years of trying to stand on her own feet, La Meri's heart began to seek some sources outside the bitter-sweet joy of creation.

Frantically I took up smoking and cocktails and assiduous nightclubbing. Every night after the curtain went down in my theatre I rushed out of the town, gleefully squired by men of any and all ages and any and all financial brackets. For a little while it was all delicious never, never land and I was happy as a sub-deb.

She then turned back to her old love, poetry and spent lonely moments writing them down with her affectionate pet Topsy curled against her feet.

There was the welcome diversion of her 'Exotic Ballet' being engaged at Jacob's Pillow as a resident company which turned out to be hectic indeed. In the midst of rushing around the States for concerts, giving classes, etc., she had to face the death of her favourite Uncle Ben. He was a strange man and they were taken aback to hear that he left quarter of million dollars to his four nieces. 'I vowed at that time that the theatre would not eat up Uncle Ben's legacy as it had Pappy's and I have kept that vow'.

She now focussed her attention on young artistes who aimed towards ethnic dance concert work. She provided them the facility and gave half of the gate collection too. Many of them who were presented by her, made successful dance careers. She had to travel frequently and to faraway places and she did this because, 'You have to feel deeply, that you are bringing something of beauty or understanding to the people out front; it is that which keeps one at it. Believe me, for pure self-aggrandizement, it is not worth it; and that is why so many give up after a few years.'

Soon La Meri's wanderlust struck her again. She with a small group emplaned to Mexico hoping to find a solution to her problems. Here she presented three full programmes of 'on stage dressing room', which when she tried out earlier elicited favourable responses. It consisted of a little dressing room with table and costume rack placed upstage centre behind the cyclorama. After each dance she went into the dressing room and chatted with the audience as she donned the next costume. Here she suffered three impacted teeth which had to be extracted: 'Happily for vanity and aesthetics the teeth were all in the back. I left Mexico part Mexican, via new teeth'. As usual, her tour was packed with adventures and problems but it was a success. In addition, in Panama, they compared her to Pavlova, Argentina and Argentinita. However, the political unrest in this region made her cut short her tour.

'During the twenty-four hour flight from Peru to New York, I gingerly re-examined the unrest that had been nagging me when I began the tour. In spite of the warm success my little tour had enjoyed, I could tell that the era of the solo dance was finished abroad as well as in the States'. With changing world, the demands of the theatre were changing; the booker, more interested in quantity than quality, was demanding large companies carrying complete decor and using full orchestra. La Meri also found that financially they were at a very dangerous low and the students did not stay on to keep up the activities. They parted to earn a living elsewhere. She engaged Ruby Cunningham as a receptionist. It is to this, her dedicated help and others like her, she managed to float. 'Without their faith and help I could not have gone on fighting for the ideal in which I so believed'.

The television was opening up a new venue for dancers while the others were shrinking. Though it may be a financial solution for the company, she felt a misfit for it. She felt 'dance is an emotional duet between artiste and audience, one cannot perform a duet alone.

She then joined with De Falco to go for concerts. During this time she met Ruth who gave her sound friendly advice when she literally wept saying, 'I cannot give up the fight to bring my little spot of culture to my country'. Ruth said, '... Indeed I have watched you and you must give it. But it need not necessarily be from behind footlights'. 'So I thought about it, to give knowledge and inspiration and...the theatre in my country might be floundering, but education was flourishing, everyone was interested in education... learning had almost become an idol. Very well, then, I would storm the fortress of the future with the materials of education. Suddenly I was happy again. I had a new dream, a new hope and new plans to make'.

It was very fortuitous that at this moment the Jowa State University asked La Meri to give a course and so she plunged into haunting the libraries, between the classes and quizzing her fellow teachers on a range of pedagogical approaches. In her Dance Centre, background lectures became a routine and she increased her teaching schedule, by giving classes in dance techniques, ethnic dance, history and culture as well as choreography, music fundamentals, pedagogy and costume design. She pointed out that in a Javanese or Spanish dance they were not just being Javanese or Spanish, but were expressing through movement, which study had made natural a living emotion common to all mankind. She said, 'I was obsessed with the desire to pass on to these groping young people the understanding and growth which the years had brought me.' Suddenly the ethnic dance series at the museum closed and the Joseph's Manns series which promoted avant-garde dance closed and she was hit badly by this. So she turned her interest to create for Theatre Dance Incorporation and The Choreographer's Workshop. But they also ceased to exist. Amidst these dance deaths, Jacob's Pillow managed to stand proudly and grow. She went there to teach and create and participate in choreographic, works and went on a long tour along with a group of distinguished artistes. She went on juggling with her time and programmes, because she needed money to keep up the Centre. She created a ballet on Vivaldi's four seasons and she found this very eminently satisfying.

I was elated with the audience and the critics' reaction. But the cherry on the cake came when Antony Tudor, greatest of ballet choreographers and never one to give compliments lightly - gave it his unqualified approval. Whatever else I have or have not gained in my life, these are my riches, the approval of such towering figures as Coomaraswamy, Argentinita, Pearl Buck, Kriesler Respighi and others of like stature.

She suffered from a severe allergic condition and she realised it may be the hair dye. She was touring with De Falco who was on the sunny side of thirty and she felt she would look like his grandmother dancing around with him. After a harrowing tour she said, 'Peter, I've had it. I am tired driving through floods and snowstorms and hurricanes—this dust-storm is the last straw. From here on it's all yours, you are young, you can take it. Get yourself another partner, or a little company. I hand you the torch. You carry it'.

Now she was desperately thinking of the next stage where she could make enough money for the Centre. She conceived the idea of the 'Little Show'. 'As a theme I took the story of my career, for laughs — that commodity so prized by American audiences. I would relate my experiences studying in foreign lands, making myself the stupid one, who could not comprehend anything'. Though the theatre business liked the idea, many others who thought of her as an erudite and serious artiste were very disturbed with it. So the show did not financially help the Centre, which finally closed down in 1956. From 1939 to 1956, she had nurtured it with care and devotion.

'The Little Show'

The summum bonum of the Centre, I believe, has been less in the education it has given than in the levels it has enriched. There are those who say that I have changed the face of the dance in America. I hope this is true, for my deepest personal desire has been to advance the culture of my country. At least I have given a new word to dance vocabulary. 'Ethnic' dance now stands side by side with 'ballet' and 'modern'. Besides my dozen graduates, there are many young people who are better world citizens because they have studied and understood the cultures of other peoples. The theme song of my life had been seeking the battle, setting myself the nearly unaccomplishable task to accomplish. I must learn now, where I am needed, doors will open for me and I must find work which awaits me by walking through these doors and finding it.

She even toured again with Ram Gopal and danced in Latin America in 1958.

There is still so much I want to do. I want to gather all I know of ethnic dance into one big volume, prodigally using my millions of notes on the subject. I want to continue to help new, young dancers to carry on the work of bringing the aesthetic wisdom of older dance-arts to the enrichment of America; and I want to make aware of these young artistes, works.

Thus she went on and did not feel as if she had grown older but only grown up: 'No more do I furiously resent being misunderstood, being regarded as someone rich, playing at dancing; or a good-time girl, on a hunt for a new kind of glamour. Now I find such ideas comical and am grateful for the unerring panacea of laughter'.

Russel Meriwether Hughes was a vibrant colourful person intent on learning many skills and arts. Surprisingly enough, she did very well in all of them whether it was horse riding, swimming, singing, Mexican dancing or poetry writing. She gradually became the dancer La Meri as she learnt more about the dances, the world and her own innermost feelings. Carreras played a very big role in promoting La Meri as a soloist and he supported her in all her activities. He gave her practical as well as intellectual help and guidance. It is unfortunate that their marriage did not last. It is also obvious that Lilian, La Meri's sister, was a close friend and a strong pillar of support. They shared many joys and sorrows together. Besides, Lilian's financial support helped La Meri and her students to continue with their activities.

2

IMAGES
La Meri and the Indian Imagery

Within La Meri was a hidden longing for something new which was sparked off by seeing Indian dance. It not only visually stimulated her into learning Indian dance movements but also compelled her to think deeply about the inner significance of dance and its great potential for human development.

It is interesting to note how a foreigner studied Indian classical dances and found ways and means of learning them effectively in a short duration of time. As an outsider feeling from 'inside', she could sense the spiritual evolution of the self while learning and performing these dances. She was most impressed by the hand gestures and facial expressions which communicated the entire range of feelings from the natural to the profane. She supplemented her acquired skills in Indian dance by reading various books. *Natyashastra* to her (as it is for all of us here in India), was an encyclopaedia on body movements and expressions. So she used *Natyashastra* as a manual for teaching her courses as we shall see in the later chapters.

During her formative years as a dancer, between 1927 and 1933, she toured widely giving concerts and learning various dances in places they stopped over. She spent three years in Paris (1930-33) and during these years she saw Uday Shankar in a concert.

> This was my utterly glamorous introduction to Indian dance. I got acquainted with Shankar and his company. I asked him to teach me, but he replied he did not teach and suggested I come to all his rehearsals and steal whatever I could. He gave me recordings and Coomaraswamy's book of mudras. So I made my first Indian dance (*Lasyanatana*) which Uday Shankar looked at, corrected and okayed. I danced *Lasyanatana* in India and it was very well received.

Thus inspired and fortified La Meri, when she came to India had two lucky breaks. Firstly Mr G.K. Seshagiri, secretary of the Rennaisance Theatre in Madras introduced her to a Bharatanatyam dance performance and to Sri Papanasam Vadivelu Pillai, who agreed to teach her Bharatanatyam. Secondly, she had a meeting with the young Ram Gopal who was keen on spreading his wings outside India. They both formed a

A girl

To drink

To speak

Namaste

Hand Gestures of La Meri

Plucking flower

Being united

The lotus and the bee

Dance posture

Hand Gestures of La Meri

symbiotic relationship from which both benefited. She, by learning more Indian classical dance techniques and he by learning about stage presentation, make-up, costuming and production techniques and by exposure to foreign audiences.

Inspired by Indian dance and her experiences, La Meri went back to USA and met Ruth St. Denis who acted as a catalyst in making La Meri take up teaching Indian dance to Americans. Thus was born Natya School of Indian dance which played a very successful and significant role in introducing Indian dance to American audiences. It was sheer hard work and belief in the usefulness of her programme that kept her going, surmounting numerous hardships and hurdles.

She developed a deep understanding of Indian dance forms which she held in high esteem. As she said in one of her lectures:

> If you study the dance expressions of a race, you come very close to the true soul, the true aspirations of the race. All that a folk desires to be expressed in the typical dance, is the result of centuries of emotional expressions by the race itself.
>
> If you are asked what is Indian dance?, the answer to that is, 'it is the most complete dance art'. If you are asked, 'why do Indians dance?', the answer is 'to worship God'. If you are asked, 'what sort of thing is Indian dance?' the answer is, 'it is visually beautiful, scientifically accurate, intellectually complete and spiritually exalted'. If you are told, 'that sounds like too much for me', the answer is 'if you search for the key it is in the shadow pictures that children make on the wall, on the little games your mother taught you'.
>
> Indian dance has the advantage of teaching students the ability to move different parts of the body for expressing and moving and it also develops muscular strength and flexibility. The spiritual growth of the student of Hindu dance is so gentle, so unstudied that she is scarcely aware of it herself. Yet after a short time of studying this spiritual art, she acquires a sort of spiritual stillness, an inner column of peace around which all else moves. I repeat, this rare spiritual gentleness is gained unconsciously by the student, yet after a certain period of study others begin to notice in the subject a calmness, a lack of nerves, a generosity of spirit, a spiritual sincerity, a soft voice, a finer manner, in short, a soul which having found itself is at peace with itself and the world.

(The above is quoted from the speech made by La Meri at the East and West Teachers Course on 29 April 1943. *The Dance of India.*)

La Meri wrote in her diary,

> When I first went to India I toured as a concert soloist and in the great storehouse of the treasured *Natyashastra*, I sought materials for solos of beauty for my own repertoire as a dancer. But immediately I was enmeshed in the spell of a science which is at once a vast and complicated technique and a pure kinetic truth. Thus my studies far over reached the original egoistic one of personal repertoire to embrace the knowledge of truth for truth's sake. I have never lost my first vast wonderment of this art and I trust that I may pass on to the uninitiated the same respect and awe which this science holds for me.... and India that richest of mines for the researches. How much she has already taught the West? How much her ancient knowledge you are already using without even knowing it and yet the surfaces barely scratched?

She cited some of the infinite choreographic riches :

- Attack oppositional in Bharatanatyam
- Attack circular in Kathakali

- Technique of joints
- Demonstration of whole theme using hands and face
- Defined lines and stances

In one of the lectures she said, 'To my way of thinking, the most complete and satisfying form of solo dance art, we find in Bharatanatyam. A multifaceted art with a beginning, middle and an end'.

She founded the School of Natya in New York City in 1940, along with Ruth St. Denis for teaching Indian dance to Americans. Out of the school grew The Ethnologic Center, which functioned as an academy until 1956. The study was rigorous. The following list will give an idea of the depth and span of the study:

1. Physical techniques—Four to six hours daily and was graded.
2. History and culture—Lectures and research.
3. Music—Western music, dynamics of music, movement to music. Eastern music: study of 'thalas' and learning to play the tabla.
4. Writing articles and speaking on various aspects of culture and dance.
5. Dance composition and choreography—Study of the structure and works presented on the stage.
6. Make-up, costume and production—The students were expected to do their own production.
7. Pedagogy—Lecture demonstration under supervision.

She took a lot of trouble to make the programme cohesive and meaningful. Meanwhile she herself kept searching for deeper knowledge.

She also wrote *Gesture Language of the Hindu Dance* which for that period of time was a great boon to Oriental dancers where lots of *hasta* mudras were shown in photographs along with explanations of their usage. The stances and hand positions that go with the mudras however, were not properly shown by her. Also the book does not distinguish between Bharatanatyam and Kathak. In those days, books with clear illustration of *adavus* were not available; therefore she resorted to *Natyashastra* for training in dance techniques. Also her knowledge and command over Bharatanatyam were limited, nor did she have the time to acquire deeper expertise. On the other hand, she did not miss an opportunity to learn something new from Indian artistes who visited USA.

She made a few filmstrips of her dance productions and programmes. One sees that they are well presented and well choreographed, but on the other hand, Bharatanatyam items seen, e.g. Allarippu and Thillana look different from what we now see and learn. Her associates like Matteo and Nalananjan had improved on the content as she gave them foundation to build up on. The Bharatanatyam *adavus* are not described except for: *That adavu, Nattai adavu, Tati Mettu, Arudi, Kudithumetu* in their basic forms. Her written instructions for teaching basic talas on tabla are fairly adequate. Not only did she teach them to play the tabla, she also often played the tabla for the performances of the Natya group.

She also insisted on students reading a lot of background material on Indian history, culture and mythology. She was keen that Indian ethos and aesthetics were not misrepresented. She was often asked to give lecture demonstrations and courses on this topic in various educational institutions. Besides, the Natya group along with her were invited to give Indian dance programmes.

TEACHING: HINDU DANCE TECHNIQUE

She used *Natyashastra* to teach the movements of the various parts of the body and their Sanskrit names. She followed *Tandava Lakshana* interpretations. She went into the detailed workout of *Vartanam, Vaksa Rechaka, Kaksa Rechaka, Kati Rechaka, Sthanak Stharam* resting positions and gives the explanations in a simple practical manner. She continues with asanas (seats) *Bhoumiyamandala, Pada* (floor foot positions) *Bhoumiya Caris* (steps). Some of the steps are not completely explained, e.g. for *Ancitapada* and *Kuncitapada* she explained only the side stepping for *Ancita* and back stepping for *Kuncita. Akasapada* (lifted foot positions), *Akasa Cari* (movements of leg in air), *Gati* (gaits), *Bhramari* (spirals), *Utplavana* (leaps), *Griva Rechaka* (neck movements), *Dristi* and *Darsanas* are eye movements taken from the mirror of gesture. She stressed a lot on *Mukhaja*. This is what gives rise to the holistic presentation of the mood and characterisation.

She broke up these specialised aspects of movements into simple actions with their Sanskrit terminology and then cross-linked them when she taught another form of ethnic dance which used these specific movements. She also gave as a class exercise, combinations for the students to do, which reinforced their practical knowledge and execution besides encouraging them to use their creativity and experience. This pedagogic experience she brought out in a publication 'The East Indian Dance'. (*Technique of the East Indian Dance*, Part II. Submitted by MacIntosh and Oitsy in 18 East, 41st St., New York, which served as a guide to many students.)

Out of the two sets of class routines using *Natyashastra* technique taught by her one has been mentioned below. She was systematic in developing the dance courses. This is the class routine scheduled for the beginners. Details of the courses are given in the Appendix.

HINDU TECHNIQUES[1] (Beginners)

Class Routine

Hand exercises	:	(*Shankar patakas; allapalavas*)
Hasta mudras	:	34 positions of the hands
Hasta prana	:	"Lives" or movements of the hands
Sentences	:	(One *hasta mudra* per week) walk in circle with sentence. Simple combination under same sentence.
Kati Rechaka	:	(waists)
Kaksa Rechaka	:	(shoulders)
Vartanam (arms)		

1. The terms used are as given by her in the notes.

Sthanaka stharam (plies)
Thatadavu (floor contacts) (*teya-te*)
Ayata
Kuncita
Ancita
Nikuta

Selected *adavus* (Bharatanatyam combos)
Selected Manipuri combos

NINE HASTA PRANA

1.	*Kuncita* (bent)	:	curl inward
2.	*Prerita* (direct)	:	curl backward
3.	*Recita* (circle)	:	revolved
4.	*Apavastita*	:	palm turned down—*uttara*
5.	*Udvestita*	:	palm turned up—*adhomuka*
6.	*Punkhita*	:	fluttering
7.	*Vyavrita*	:	turned back at wrist
8.	*Bhujanga* (serpent)	:	wavy movement
9.	*Prasrana*	:	relaxed and/ or separated

VARTANAM[2]

The *vartanam* (arm positions) are divided into five categories : straight, curved, bent, hanging and others. These arm positions may be combined in any way that creates beauty of air design and has *aucitya.*[3] It must be clearly understood that the position of the wrist, hands and fingers is in no way dependent upon, nor influenced by the *vartanam.*

In executing the straight arms (*suci, apaviddha, dola, akasa*), care should be taken not to lock the elbow (hyperextention) and to keep the arm in the proper position when used in combination with waist movements which tilt the upper body.

In executing the curved arms, elbows must be held in a gentle curve, with elbow bone pointing horizontally backward, not downward. The curved arms include *sadir suci, sadir apaviddha, sadir akasa* and *lata.* As in the straight arms, care must be taken to maintain the proper line of arm to shoulder when executing waist movements.

The bent arms (*kati, vaksa, kaksa* and *ganda kuncita*) are bent in the elbow to bring the hand into the region indicated. This does not mean that the hand must touch the waist, chest, shoulder or face.

The hanging arms (*gaja, udara* and *samba*) are relaxed at the elbow without hyperextension and should not disturb the shoulder.

Of the arms gathered under the fifth category, the *ardhadola* should be executed exactly with elbow at shoulder level and forearm an exact perpendicular. *Katiga* is an iconographic term, but the position is used by the Ceylonese dancers as a *sama* pose.

---

2. The terms given by her in her notes.
3. Aptness/suitableness.

The *dola* arms are performed with straight elbows and may be placed at any angle desired, straight down in front.

BHOUMIYA CARI

The *bhoumiya cari* are the movements of the leg on the earth. Loosely they might be called 'steps', but in so doing we lose the important kinetic lesson that the impetus of any step of the foot must generate in the upper thigh. So much so that *calana*, the impetus itself, is named as a *bhoumiya cari.*

Ati kranta is executed with unlocked knees, the heel and ball striking the floor simultaneously and the toes descending as the stepping foot takes the weight. It may be done from a *sama*, with toes straightforward, or from *ayata*, with toes turned out.

Parsva kranta may also be done from either *sama* or *ayata*. In *swastika*, care must be taken to turn the crossed knee and foot well-out.

Partschvakranta, janita, casa cari, kuttana, apaviddha, ardha-suci, the five lunges, *vicyava* may all be executed from either *sama* or *ayata pada*, i.e. *sama*, toes pointing forward, *ayata*, toes pointing outwards.

In *janita cari*, the heel and ball glide simultaneously, while the toes follow at the taking of the weight, as in *ati-kranta.*

In *acasa cari*, the lift of the leg is generally executed on the 'and' count and the step taken on the beat of the tala.

Kuttna may be done with either heel, half-toe or full sole as indicated. In *ancita, viksipta, purakshepa, suci-pasrta, parsvakshepa*, the extended leg should not show a fully-locked knee: the extended foot may be in any *akasa pada* desired.

In executing *eklakridita* and *udghatita*, care should be taken not to jump off the floor, but rather to slide, slightly but definitely the balls of the feet to sound the bells. The leg position is *vaicakha*; and the angle of the knees should be changed as little as possible when descending to the heels. Do not rise high on the half toes, as this shows too much bounce in the knees.

Visama should be executed from *ayata* when the body is not spiralled in moving. When the body is spiralled, *sama* is used.

Vicyava is in the nature of a two-step to the side.

To trill the bells in *stitavarta*, the following foot may be dragged on the ball of the foot, on the end of the great toe, or on the upper joint of the great toe.

Calana comes into play in every movement of the lower limbs. The impetus of a step does not start in the knee, but from the upper thigh, from the groin. It is well known that all dynamic movement starts on the torso where lies the emotional motor. Assuming that this motor is already running in the dancer before he makes any movement at all (and it must be), the first muscular reaction to a movement of the lower limbs, no matter how simple a step it may be, must be felt and sent from the upper thigh. The *calana* gives quality to movement, without which dancing becomes mere stepping about.

Here are a set of exercises for extension equilibrium, etc. These have been tried and are very practical and effective.

Sets of Exercises for Extension, Equilibrium, etc.

1. (a) From *ayata*; 2 *talagra* and *kuncita* (heels on ground)
   (b) From *ayata*; 3 *talagra* and *kuncita* (heels up)
   (c) From *ayata* : *nikuta*: extd., *nikuta, ayata.*
   From *motitam* : waist and shoulders *Rechijaka*
2. (a) From *ayata*; 3 *kuncitas* each deeper than foregoing.
   (b) From *alidha*; sweep *frt.* foot to *nikuta* and place *bk. alidha*
   (c) From *prerita*; slow *vidhutkranta*
3. (a) Limber on floor
   (b) From *ayata; ajakranta-krama* and *L*; *alata r & l*
   (c) From *sama* (in profile); *harinapluta* in *vrsak*
4. (a) Limber on floor and into asanas
   (b) From *ayata*; *aviddha* and *prata-swastikas r & l;* rept. in *talagra.*
   (c) *Danda-pada*; swing to open *nikuta.*
5. (a) From *alidha* (profile) to *sthanaka stharam*; rise to *talagra*; quarter-turn
   (b) Swinging *nupuras, frt* and *bk*
   (c) From *ayata*, *vishnukranta* and *suci-vrdha, alt.*
6. (a) From *sama*; *suci-pada fwd* to *alidha*; each foot sixteen times
   From *ayata*: *suci-pada obl.*, each foot sixteen times
   (b) *Inonikuta*, bend; standing leg twice, on third, *entd*; half toe; *rep alt.*
   (c) *Vishnukranta*; extend with knee bent, then straighten knee *gra* and *ret.*
7. (a) From *prenkhana*; *avarta* (*suci* and *padograta*) and *ret.* to *prenkhan.*
   (b) *Vrsaka* turning slowly ("flying" of Chidambaram)
   (c) *Vrsaka*; erect and lowering at pelvis.
9. (a) From *sama*; bend knees and *suci-pada fwd*
   From *ayata* : bend knees and *suci-pada* oblique
   (b) Swing from *urdvu-janu* to *vrsaka* twice; turn in *vrsaka*
   (c) *Vidhutkranta* finishing in *aindra*
10. (a) From *prekhana*; *aksipta*
    (b) *Prenkhana* on *talagra*; hold and into *aviddha*
    (c) *Ajakranta-krama* (half round)
11. (a) From *prerita*; twice *talagra* and into *vaisnava*
    (b) From *urdvu-janu* to *vrasaka* and onto *talagra*

---

alt.	=	alternate
extd.	=	extend
frt and bk	=	front and back
fwd	=	forward
gra	=	gradually
L	=	Left
obl.	=	oblique
pt. fwd.	=	point forward
r & l	=	Right and Left
rep alt.	=	repeat alternate
rept.	=	repeat
ret.	=	return

(c) *Ajakranta-krama* into *nikuta; talagra*

12. (a) From *sama*; *kuncita*; straighten knees and pt. fwd. on floor
From *sama* : same at ankle
From *sama* : same at knee
Repeat from *ayata*

(b) In *swastike talagra*; two *kampita dkati* and into *danda-pada*

(c) *Alata*; onto *nikuta* and *talagra*

13. (a) From *ayata*; *vaisnava*; "grind" and up

(b) *Danda-pada*; slow turn with heel-beats

(c) *Nupura* (kick) and into plunge

14. (a) Rhythmic, swining *motitams* from Kathakali

(b) From *ayata*; *talagra* on both; on twice; on 1 twice; rest 2 counts.

Prof. V. Raghavan who is an authority on *Natyashastra* and music, used to send La Meri various articles of interest on these subjects and so did A.K. Coomoraswamy. She collected various cuttings on topics of interest. Besides, she had a good collection of pictures from different magazines, related to the art, topography, dance, music, costumes and traditions of many countries. Thus she was able to give courses on Indian culture in universities and colleges, besides her own institution. Similarly, she had a vast knowledge of Latin American culture. As a teacher and an educator, she achieved much more than any of her contemporaries. As mentioned earlier, her books on : *The Gesture Language of the Hindu Dance*, *Spanish Dancing* and *Dance Composition*, are still being used by young dancers in USA. The book on dance composition is indeed useful for students all-over the world. The total education on ethnic dance is an eye-opener for anyone who wants to try out a new dance vocabulary or format.

La Meri with students performing Bharatanatyam

Group programme in Bharatanatyam

Within Technique, as presented by La Meri, offers ideas and methodology for those who want to train on contemporary Indian modern/Indian ballet-styles. She was a true pedagogue in the best sense.

CHOREOGRAPHY

The creative possibilities inherent in the Indian dance are almost limitless. In 1944, she staged *Swan Lake* on the Indian dance idiom. She says, 'I could not believe the stir this ballet caused in the dance field and certainly I could never have guessed that twenty-five years later Matteo would restage this work with his Indo-American Company and that it would again cause something of a furore. Echoes were heard even in India and *Span* magazine of November 1970 devoted a story and a cover to Matteo's production'.

She also choreographed *Bach Bharata* to the music of Bach. Though this did not get the same popularity as *Swan Lake*, it was a very good composition. It is an interesting piece, but not an exciting one. Besides, the style here was diluted because it was a melange of Kathak, Bharatanatyam and creative dance.

La Meri says that it was a chance meeting with Anatole Chujoy which encouraged her in plunging into the *Swan Lake* production, mainly to illustrate the great clarity of Indian gestures when applied to a well-known story.

> The technique of Hindu *natya* is so complete that the thrill of pirouettes and leaps need not necessarily be eschewed, but without introduction one step or posture which has not been classified in the palm leaf manuscript of the past which deals with this complete art science, one may follow the general lines of the ballet as laid down by Petipa, display physical technique and yet not lose the story itself. Mindful that some may doubt the authenticity of some of these steps, I have written down the choreography with the Sanskrit technical terms and any balletomane may check them against the steps which they have seen, while any student who has completed the Diploma in Classical Hindu Dance will find the text clear to restage this ballet exactly as you have seen it here.

Unfortunately her writings on this theme are not in the collection available at IGNCA. It would have been very interesting to visualise *Swan Lake* presented using the format and principles of Bharatanatyam and *Natyashastra*.

The following pages will give glimpses of various dances and choreographed pieces La Meri composed for herself and for the Natya group. It is amazing how she managed to choreograph so many items. The reviews of her performances and productions are flattering of her choreographic abilities. This also favourably reflects her capacity to teach effectively the intricacies of Indian dance techniques and sentiments. She had shown grit in tackling challenging choreographic pieces like *Bach Bharata*, Verdi's *Four Seasons* and Rimsky-Korsokov's *Scheherazade*, where she has used Indian dance movements to western classical music.

The review of the performances were very good and balanced.

Swan Lake

Music by: Peter Tchaikowsky; *Translated by:* La Meri into the dance-idiom of India after the choreography of Marius Petipa; *Costumes:* La Meri and G. Carreras; *Lights and Sound:* Averardo Bertocchi

...La Meri and her company of fourteen appeared in a repeat performance of her Hindu dance version of Swan Lake. *After many seeings, the choreography remains utterly enchanting and still appears to be, in many ways superior to the balletic version. La Meri gave a radiant performance as the 'Swan Queen'.*

Walter Terry—*New York Herald Tribune*

...The story of Swan Lake comes forth in La Meri's version with much greater coherence and clarity than in any other production.... This simple plot is complete in every detail, unfolds with every subtle nuance.... La Meri's Swan Lake *is an excellent show, good theatre...a most interesting, most valuable and courageous experiment....*

Anatole Chujoy—*Dance News*

... For this may well be the first step in a slow but rich evolution, a new deepening, of the western art of the dance....

Joseph T. Shipley—*New Leader*

...An artistic achievement...one of the boldest experiments in the history of the dance art.... There is genius in the simplicity of this idea.... The most critical moment came when the first notes of the sweet and nostalgic first valse began. One felt that this was the most critically dangerous moment. A valse "a la Hindu?" Yes sir, a valse a la Hindu. The daring experiment was a success !...

Felix Cleve—*Staats-Zeitung und Herold*

Krishna-Gopala

Music by: Vishnu Dass Shirali; *Choreography and Costumes :* La Meri; *Decor:* George Duberg; *Lights and Sound:* Averardo Bertocchi

...Not since Shankar himself have we seen anything Oriental as delicately beautiful as the Krishna-Gopala *ballet of La Meri. In it she gave new proof of the versatility of her artistry.*

Albertine Citak—*Dance*

It is for beauty of dance and the diversified rhythms of the music (on native recordings) rather than dramatic significance that one admires La Meri's Natya repertoire....

Robert Lawerence
—*New York Herald Tribune*

... An Indian ballet, Krishna-Gopala *(Lasya Natya), choreographed by La Meri.... The story was taken from a pastoral drama by Jaidev,* Gita Govinda *and the entire work resulted in a clear dance story which had excellent movement, clarity of design and color. The point is that La Meri has demonstrated the theatrical and emotional richness of the Indian dance as a source of dance stories (ballets) that can appeal to the American public without false pretension....*

F.X.G.—*Dance*

Scheherazade

Music by: Rimsky-Korsakov; *Choreography by:* La Meri; *Costumes Designed by:* Ethnologic Dance Center; *Decor, Lights and Sound:* Averardo Bertocchi.

...I saw her version in Indian dance form of Scheherazade *and found it infinitely more exciting than the weary balletic version which we have seen for so many seasons. If you think that Hindu dance is limited to hand gestures, then I advise you to see the Hindu leaps and spins which give virtuosic verve to La Meri's lush* Scheherazade....

Walter Terry
—*New York Herald Tribune*

...One of...La Meri's...most fruitful and balanced works...lively and entertaining production with engaging charm and rousing beauty...variegated stir of color and lively form....

Joseph T. Shipley—*New Leader*

...The choreography is a coherent, altogether satisfactory expression of Rimsky-Korsakov's music Scheherazade, *measure for measure.... The performance is both refreshing and intelligent....*

R. Wade—*Dance*

Gauba's Journey to Paradise

Music by: Wasantha Wana Singh; *Choreography and Costumes:* La Meri; *Lights and Sound:* Averardo Bertocchi

...Gauba's Journey to Paradise *is well conceived ... it was a creditable showing, excellently rehearsed and lavishly costumed....*

John Martin—*New York Times*

...The American dancer has been able to delve deeply into the folklore of India and in the three works presented she expressed the rituals and fantastic (to Americans) dances in a style that was near perfection. Every movement of her lithe, swaying body, every sensuous movement of her hands, every expression, from coyness and joy to mad horror, were vividly depicted. She received a deserved ovation....

Variety

...La Meri and her remarkable group staged a series of divertissements followed by a Hindu ballet punctuated by humorous situations, not usually expected in the Hindu classic dance. It was called Gauba's Journey to Paradise *and was danced to the very hilt by the group and masterfully illustrated by word of mouth in a preface by La Meri, who, in her role as the Celestial Elephant, caused considerable excitement among the audience....*

The American Dancer

Iberia

Music by : Debussy; *Choreography by :* La Meri on indications of the composer; *Costumes :* Juan Beaucaire-Montalvo; *Lights and Sound :* Averardo Bertocchi

...The presentation of Debussy's Iberia *was a happy thought. The music is eminently suited to dancing and Madame La Meri invented for it an interesting scenario and staged to it excellent dances....*

Anatole Chujoy–*Dance News*

...Sumptuous work in three scenes set to Debussy's Iberia....

Rosalyn Krokover–*Musical Courier*

... A beautiful and colorful characterization....

R. Wade–*Dance*

... A dainty, classical Spanish dance narrative...a colorful stageful of dancers....

R.V.H.–*The Evening Eagle*

Devi Murti

Music by: Wana Singh of Vishnu Dass Shirali;
Choreographed by: La Meri; *Décor by:* Guido Carreras;
Lights and Sound by: Averardo Bertocchi

...Devi Murti *is one of La Meri's finest pieces and something of a tour de force for this great star...*

La Meri's characterizations were dramatically powerful and there was a good deal more physical action than one expects of the Hindu dance. As the Wife, La Meri was softly amorous in her dancing, swaying, swirling her skirts, insinuating her body through the measures of dance. Turning to powerful movements, she revealed the aspect of the goddess of battle and finally, with streaming hair and frightening fangs, she danced the role of the Destroyer. As the Teacher, she touched her role a deity with quiet kindliness and, as the abstract form of the goddess, she evoked the quality of serene dignity....

Walter Terry—*New York Herald Tribune*

...La Meri admirably dances the five aspects...offering a whole gamut of moods and exhibiting five beautiful costumes....

Anatole Chujoy—*Dance News*

...Devi Murti, *all of the aspects of the Supreme Goddess are exalted (and thrillingly theatrical).*

H.D.—*The American Dancer*

El Amor Brujo

Music by: Manual de Fall; *Choreographed by:* La Meri; *Décor by:* Guido Carreras & Duberg; *Costumes by:* La Meri & Guido Carreras; *Lights and Sound by:* Averardo Bertocchi

...Of all the productions of Amor Brujo I have seen—and these include versions by Argentina, Esudero, Woizikowski and Argentinita, that presented by La Meri is much the most consistent and satisfactory from a dramatic viewpoint. This is due to the humility—and wisdom—of the producers in letting the work speak for itself instead of using it as an instrument for the display of the star's abilities.

Anatole Chujoy—*Dance News*

...Life-like and alluring picture, full of atmosphere and soul stirring drama....

Felix Cleve—*Staats-Zeitung und Herold*

Bach Bharata Suite

Music by: J.S. Bach; *Choreography & Costumes by:* La Meri; *Lights and Sound by:* Averardo Bertocchi

...La Meri's successful mating of Bach with the Hindu dance supplies still further proof, if such be needed, of the universality and timelessness of art, of the potential power of dance to find common denominators for supposedly alien forms and cultures.... The choreography of the Bach-Bharata Suite *gives visual being to the formal structures of the musical pieces, but more important is the reflection of the dignity and discipline inherent in the music. The choreographic craftsmanship, then, is excellent but La Meri has added to this the glow and the excitement of art by selecting her dance vocabulary with an eye to movement expressiveness, beauty of pattern and dynamic properties...a fine dance creation... ...La Meri's* Bach-Bharata Suite *is a magnificent dance work.*

Walter Terry—*New York Herald Tribune*

...With great simplicity and clarity...La Meri...composed a beautiful suite of stylized dances admirably suitable to and in full harmony with, the Bach music....

Anatole Chujoy—*Dance News*

...A triumph of mathematical precision in the pattern of the choreography....

D.S.—*Dance*

...Latest and loftiest work...

Margaret Lloyd
—*Christian Science Monitor*

3

CRYSTALS
La Meri as an Ethnic Dance Expert

La Meri was popularly known as the greatest 'ethnic dancer'. In fact she was the one who introduced the term 'ethnic dance' in 1940s to distinguish the dances of different nationalities from classical ballet and modern dance. It was with great zeal and zest that she studied various traditional dances and the culture of the countries she visited. It is commendable that she managed to do all this during her short trips and danced a full repertoire of ethnic dances, with perfect reproduction of the dance pieces, characterisation and costumes. As was expressed by Ram Gopal, who had a fairly long association with her, 'she switched from one face to another with ease to portray the authentic picture and form'. One could say that she crystalised the essence of each dance form so as to perform and teach it with clarity.

Besides being an expert 'ethnic dancer' she proved to be a truly great teacher of these dances. Her forte was her ability to simplify and analyse all the dance movements to perfection and to put together the music and choreography. One can say that she devoted her entire life to promote ethnic dance. La Meri, in the Preface of *Total Education in Ethnic Dance*, says:

> For some reason known only to Siva, who orchestrated the cosmic dance of the universe, all the facets of my career seem to have been preparing me for the role I have found myself playing during the past fifty odd years. It seems I have been cast in the character of explainer, and it is my destiny to reduce to a common denomination the complicated techniques and backgrounds of the various aspects of many dance arts and dance sciences.
>
> Indeed, I am most humbly honoured to be one small instrument in handing down a tradition that may be the ultimate salvation of the human race—for the art of ethnic dance is neither amusement nor a means of self-expression. As the pundits have taught us, it is a means to taste 'rasa' (sentiment or feeling—and eventually to find God).

Ethnic dance covers an unwieldy majority of the world's choreography, yet in the Orient this term ethnic dance proves so inexact as to be useless. Ethnic dance itself

Ethnic Dance Arts : La Meri with Drums

has several forms. Basic folk dances performed in the community on specific occasion, on being presented on the stage, becomes 'art dance' according to her categorisation. Art dances include dances created for worship, e.g. Hindu dance, Hula, Javanese Wayang Wang, Noh, Flamenco, etc. This, when adapted to the stage, can become one of the following :

1. Traditional—when the same dance is being performed.
2. Authentic—when time movement, etc., are curtailed.
3. The creative or neoclassic like Uday Shankar and Ram Gopal presented to the West.
4. Creative departures—technique may remain same but music could be alien and technique mixed.
5. Applied techniques—here the traditional techniques are applied to alien themes, music, costume and motivation.

La Meri believed that ethnological dance was not a product of mind but of emotions. Style is its essence and technique is of purely relative importance.

In *Total Education in Ethnic Dance*, she says,

> The body is the instrument through which the dancer speaks. He/she must understand the infinite subtleties of which the anatomy is capable. While strengthening the muscles for the rigors of 'teconeo' and 'thaat', he must also train wrists and neck and eyes to respond. Isodora Duncan declared that all expressive movements had impetus in the solar plexus. Francois Delsarte, in his study of physical expression, discovered that all spiritual and intellectual movement occurred in the upper parts of the body. The science of Bharatanatyam puts all expressive movements in the arms and hands and head and upper torso—a theory the entire Orient shares. Bharatanatyam has produced the most complete breakdown of the torso, so a consistent study of the Hindu exercises of these parts is of inestimable value to the Dancer.

Actually she was talking about *Natyashastra*, for in her classes she used many *karnas*, *hasta* mudras, and movements of *anga* and *pratyanga* for exercises and also to teach other forms of ethnic dance. For example, she found that those who had learnt *hasta* mudras made better castanet players in Spanish dancing and could easily learn other dances like the Indonesian, Hawaiian Hula and Japanese dance. Indian dance techniques based on each and every articulation, are as quick and subtle as yoga in building the muscle and strength without much strain, especially when they are used together.

THE TEACHER

Being a dancer and having learnt various dances from various teachers during a short span of time, helped her to identify numerous movements of the different parts of the body. She confesses to have learnt a lot from the *Natyashastra* and she used it as a vehicle to relate and train in other national styles.

Her uniqueness comes from the fact that she learnt to dance many authentic dances from various parts of the world, in the country of its origin and from renowned teachers. Being a gifted and ethusiastic dancer, she felt the urge to pass on her knowledge to

Hula Hands

Cambodian Hands

Speaking Hands

others for she believed that to learn from older civilisations with a more complete science of physical expression would enrich creative dance.

She gradually developed a total education programme in ethnic dance, with the objective of acquainting students with the dance forms of the Orient (India, Java, Burma, Arabia, China, Japan, Siam) and of Spain, Hawaii (Polynesia) and Latin America, and to help in understanding the social and religious mores which have influenced dance, and by strengthening the same by learning the history of dances and their correlated arts.

In my half-century of intensive study of many ethnic dance forms, I have found that there are physical controls and dynamic qualities which are built into the techniques of various types of art-forms. In western dance-arts many of these qualities (physical controls and dynamic qualities) are not taught, but are left to the instinctive artistry of the performer. I believe that these physical controls can be taught and that the dynamic controls can be awakened. Furthermore I believe that in these techniques are many seeds from which the creative modern dancer could select those upon which to build an entire school of movement, such as the fall-recovery which was the seed of Doris Humphrey's school.

La Meri selected some specialised individual characteristic techniques from each dance style to build a curriculum which would enable the dancer to dance and perform unrelated ethnic dances with certain ease and confidence. For example in India, a student

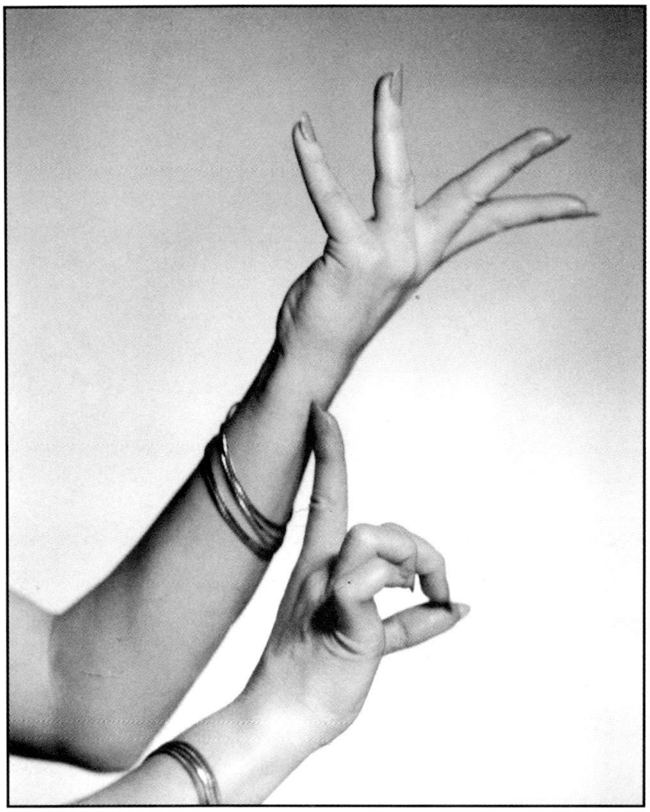

Indian Hands

Spanish Hands

Speaking Hands

of Bharatanatyam if taught Manipuri would be unable to adapt him/herself to it for a very long time and (vice versa) because he/she is taught specifically only certain body movements and positions, like the stiff *aramandi* (demiplie) stretched out hands making crystalline geometric formations with firm steppings. The hip is immobilised, the spine is straight, etc., while Manipuri demands the movement of the neck, waist, hands, etc., with smooth flow and no direct showing of expressions on the face. In a way it is taboo to do the brisk movements and expressions which is characteristic of Bharatanatyam.

Chinese Hands

On the other hand if one learnt from the beginning the various possible movements of the body, it would be easier to build on them. Thus in her curriculum, La Meri took a holistic approach to teaching

La Meri : Performing a Marwari Dance

these dance forms by training the body to acquire the skills to execute various movements along with the ethos and historical and sociological interplay.

The main points of interest in the course she created have been discussed below.

It included physical as well as mental control. Physical control : many forms of western dance neglect entirely, or make subservient, the upper body stressing the development of lower limbs. The study included (a) torso, (b) hands and wrists, (c) arms, (d) feet (arch, ankle and toes). Mental control : (a) imagination and identification, (b) motivation and dynamic quality, (c) movements in space, (d) emotional levels, and (e) relaxed control.

Her work on the spine's posture for different racial dances won a lot of admiration. It was very perceptive and clever of her to work on them. She also used some of the exercises that Uday Shankar used for his troupe.

A few examples of the class routine are given below to explain her meticulous study and understanding of movements and their significance in the dance.

Physical Control : Feet
The foot should be expressive in itself.
Let us move the ankle in all possible ways, spread and relax the toes.

Lift the arch with or without the toes pointed, and above all, feel the sole of the foot to be as expressive as the palm of the hand.

One should be able to dance on, under or above the ground, to caress the earth or strike it in anger–(and Not to be gingerly unacquainted with it).

Feel the ground–with the ball of the toes, the ball of the foot, with the heel.

EXERCISES

A. SITTING ON FLOOR

1. Point toe and ankle : pull toe and ankle upward (alternating).
2. Point toe (and ankle); place soles of feet together.
3. Spread toes; relax foot.

B. STANDING

1. 'A' exercises, alternate feet.
2. Lift foot to ankle of standing foot; lower toe first, to ground besides standing foot. *Rep. alt.* and gradually speed into slow trot.
3. In fourth position, shift weight from front to back foot, passing through locked knees, *rep. alt.*

C. WALKS

1. Hindu : (in passing, the foot glides on half toe and heel).
2. Cat feet : (lift past ankle and lower in succession of toe, ball heel).
3. Java : (with heel and ball on floor, foot passes thru, second and fourth).[1]
4. Java 'fly' (tiny, fast steps on half toe).

---

1. Position 1st, 2nd, 3rd, and 4th are the normal ballet positions.

Japan
Amer-Ind
Africa
East Indian
Bharata Natyam
Orissi
Kathakali

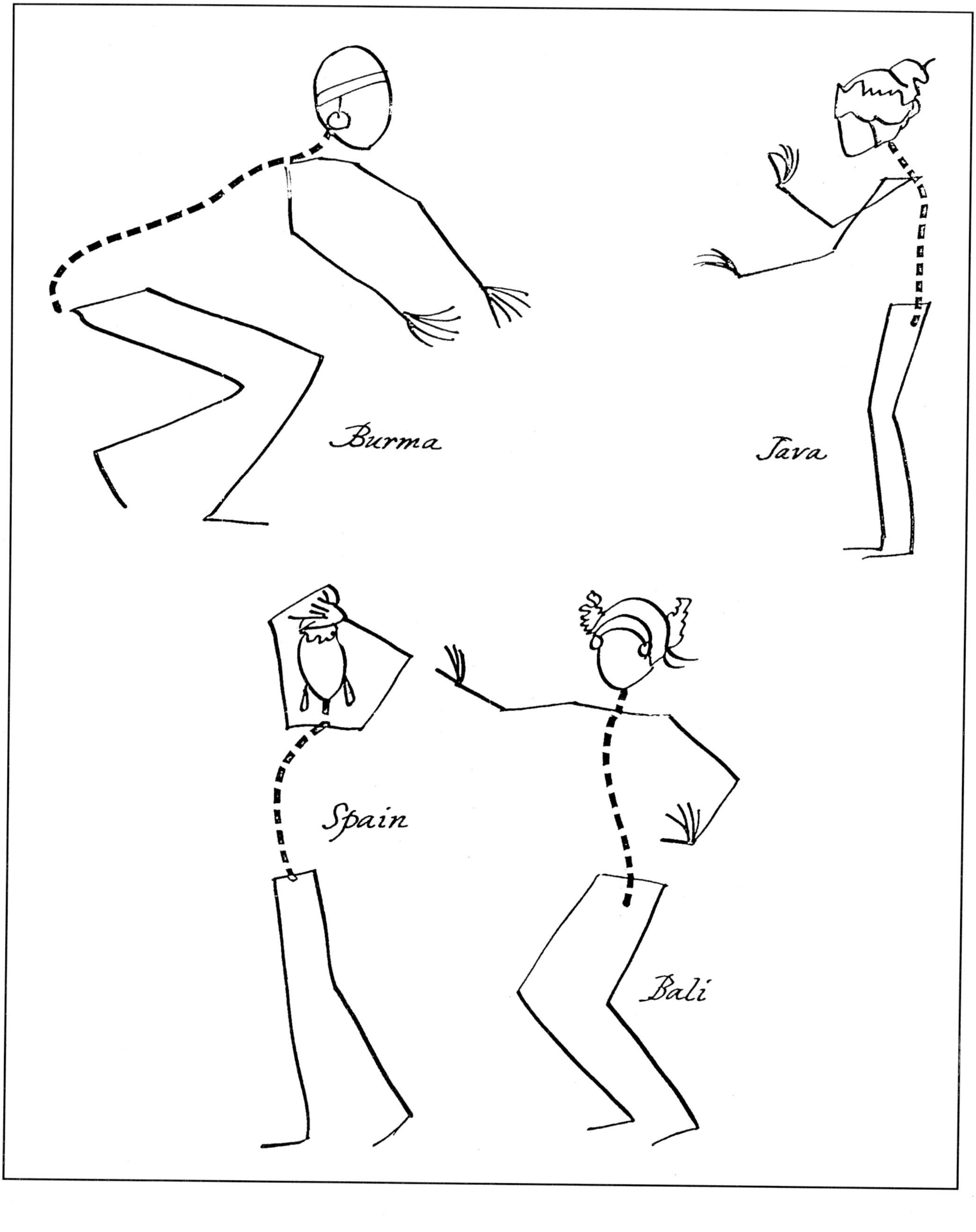
Burma
Java
Spain
Bali

La Meri Performing a Siamese Dance

5. Thai : (from first to open fourth with heel and ball touching : both knees bent).
6. Thai ('fly') : (quick, small steps with flat of foot on ground).
7. Japan (fem) : (toes in, knees together: foot passes, tight, to fourth).
8. Japan (mas) : (toes forward : foot passes : heel advances : palm down).
9. Ballet (toe first).

D. BEATS (SOFT KNEES MUST BE MAINTAINED)

1. Flat foot : slap (Kathak) : thud (Japan): dig in (Spanish).
2. Ball of foot : dig in thud.
3. Heel : dig in : strike.

E. COMBOS

1. Kathak beat and slap.
2. Bharatanatyam toes, heels, etc.
3. Flamenco toe, heel, flat, etc.

F. HANDS AND WRISTS

Next to the face, the hands are the most expressive part of the anatomy. Emotional strength, or lack of it, are shown most clearly in hands and wrists.

We do everything with our hands : why leave them out of dance expressions?

American dance puts great stress on technique of the legs; indicative of vitality, but not of thought.

(I have found very little expression in hands and wrists of students.)

All Oriental dance have a hand language although the richest and most complete is that of India.

The wrist is the thermometer of vital force.

The thumb is vital; the palm, emotional; the fingers, intellectual.

EXERCISES

HANDS

1. Tension relaxation : (Flat palm to hanging hand) (*pataka* to *prasarana*)
2. Closed tension to open tension (first to spread) (*musti* to *alapadma*)
3. Fingers in and out, beginning with 'pinky' (*alapallava*)
4. Combine #3 with wrist pivot.
5. Ripple (with wrist make succession from wrist to finger tips).
6. Move arms with finger tip lead.

WRISTS

1. With palm down, move wrists horizontally (Kathak).
2. With palm down, move wrist vertically (understated, Japan).
3. With palm down, move wrist in inward, then outward circles.
4. Contract palm backward (Marwari).
5. Combine pivotal forearms and circular wrists.
6. Combine pivotal forearms and figure eight wrists.

It is the wrist and hand which tops the air design, or send it out into infinity. The wrist and every joint of every finger should be under control, successions in the wrist and hands of circular, perpendicular and lateral movements of the wrist; tension and relaxation of the hand (palm and fingers) as well as placement of the fingers.

La Meri : Performing Jarabe, a Mexican Dance

ARMS

Arms like legs, must feel space displacement.

Arms are more expressive than legs. They are closer to the seat of the emotions (torso) and of the intellect (head).

The elbow is the thermometer of the will. They draw in for humility, thrust out for arrogance.

The hand is intellectual; the forearm, emotional; the upper arm vital.

Elbows must be controlled with emotional communication in mind.

La Meri : Performing an Odori, Japanese Dance

POSITIONS

Curved
Straight (all taken from Indian dance)
Bent at elbow
Hanging

(The curved and straight arms can be placed in any design from the body that is possible, automatically. The bent arms can be bent at any angle to the upper arm until it becomes curved. The hanging arm cannot be 'hung' when it is above shoulder height.)

MOVEMENTS

1. Flung full arm circles (*recita*), circle inward or outward, from arm socket.
2. Controlled full arm circles (above but controlled).
3. Forearm pivot.
4. Full arm pivot (prevalent in Java and Thai dance).
5. Forearm circle (inward and outward), delineate circle with wrist, elbow as axis.
6. Ripples (add elbow to 'ripples' wrist and hand for full-ripple).

NOTES

Spanish brazeo as well as ballet are excellent examples of curved arms.
Flamenco uses the high elbow (wrist below elbow level)
Kathak uses both the bent and straight arms.
Odissi and Bharatanatyam use the hanging arm.
Bharatanatyam also uses the forearm and full arm circles.
Arm movements from Michio Ito (used in music responses) as continued in the next page.

La Meri : Performing Zandunga, a Mexican Dance

La Meri : Performing Goyescas, a Spanish Dance

1. Fingers on thighs; palm down, wrist right-angled arm curved.
2. Push, palms up, upward to below breast; arms bent.
3. Arms in place; pivot and circle wrists inward until palms face out.
4. Push forward to straight arms, palms forward.
5. Pull back to bent arms over chest, wrists crossed, palms in.
6. To bent arms, palms up, finger tips touching at hairline.
7. Push up to 'Y' straight arms, palms up.
8. Lower to hanging arms (and wrists) nearly touching side of body.

Speaking Hands

NECK AND FACE

The eye follows the hand and the heart follows the 'eye' (India). Technically, the head and eye follow the hand.

The head and eye carry the 'implied line' in dance.

When the head leads the body in movement, it signifies eagerness.

When the body leads the head in movement, it signifies reluctance.

In the *Natyashastra* (India's written compendium of dance technique) there are listed

43 'looks' (eyes) (*darsanas*)/*drishti*
7 brows (*bhru*)
13 mouths (*asya*)
6 chins (*cibuka*)

(besides movements of nose and cheeks).

(A study of these and their meanings would be of inestimable value).

Delsarte lists 405 combinations of eyes and brows; 98 of necks; and says the mouth combined with these runs into hundreds of thousands.

EXERCISES

FACE

Eyes : 1. Side to side (*pralokita*)
2. Up and down (*ullokita* and *avalokita*)
3. Roll, circular (*ugra*)

Brows: 1. Lift up (*kuncita*)
2. Frown (*patana*)
3. Flutter (*lalita*)

Mouth: 1. Small smile (*udvahi*)
2. Broad smile (*ghurna*)
3. Downward at corners (*nirbhugna*)

La Meri : Performing Pois (New Zealand)

Swan Lake

Neck:
1. Roll in circle (keeping face forward) (*recita*)
2. Side and side (*dhuta*): (perform both tensed and relaxed)
3. Up and down (*kampita*)
4. Tilt (*tryasra*)
5. Chin 'pointing' toward shoulder (*oyarakam*)
6. Chin 'pointing' toward up oblique (*tirascina*)
7. Figure 8 with chin (Java : rourou)

La Meri : As Doll (creative piece)

All the above should be done, both small and large, fast and slow.

This thought has not been put into practice even now in India by many of our teachers, though we have lived with it all along. La Meri felt that teaching and learning ethnic dance were part of an inner evolution. This is reflected in her statement,

> The guru (teacher) must be for ever changing. For the first phase he must have humour and strength as well as patience and faith. For the second, he must have knowledge, strength, skill and sympathy. For the ultimate third phase he must have courage, understanding, imagination and mysticism.

She has taught and written profusely on the first and second phases but on the third written only for herself and has been not successful in finding an acolyte who could scale the heights. She says, 'I have known these heights, and I am content'.

A study of the manifold ethnic dance movements from the physiological, psychological and sociological standpoints is tremendously rewarding. It broadens the scope of the body, mind and heart and gives to its protagonist a healthy mind in a healthy body. This is probably the reason why most of the dancers had a long life, e.g. Uday Shankar, Rukmini Devi Arundale, Ram Gopal (and even La Meri herself).

La Meri stressed that quality was the most important element of ethnic dance.

> I am trying, then, to isolate and clarify certain essences of physical movement which are inherent in a given ethnic dance art. These within techniques are applicable to any form of dance art, and I believe they can be taught to the West as well as the East. It needs only to select those elements, which are (or should be) universal, and this is the task I have set myself.
>
> I would not demand of the body any bend, stretch or leap which is not within that body's natural scope. Muscles would be taught to tone toward strength and control, but never pushed beyond nature.
>
> In the beginning, the student should be taught to feel the ground with balls of toes, ball of the feet and heal. The foot should be expressive by itself. The knees should feel the weight of the body and soul. Thigh and calf should feel the displacement of space, aware of the air through which the body moves; the arms to feel the displacement in space, in relationship

La Meri : Performing Hula, a Hawaiin Dance

La Meri : Performing Devil Dance (Ceylon)

to torso and its emotions; the face, eyes above all to be taught to mirror the emotion. The trunk is the mainspring of all movements. I am convinced that study of free dancing as I have envisaged it, would be a good help and never a hindrance to student of any other school. At the same time it will leave the student healthier, happier and more beautiful and am convinced that same education is needed for the watching world, as well as dancing world. For example, the excitement of Spanish dance, the withdrawal of Hindu dance, need not be lost because the 'steps' are not used. I believe that the free (modern, contemporary) dance can borrow a great deal from the established ethnic dance arts and be greatly enriched thereby.

Frankly I feel that in too many instances the modern dancer, afraid of life and his fellow man shuts himself away in an escapist ashram and that a good look at the humanities would put him back in touch with a world he seeks to speak to. In America everything we have, culture-wise is borrowed from old cultures. We would do well to acknowledge this and drink more deeply from the ancient spring of dance.

Richest mine of within techniques is in classical dances of India. It is an art with 3,000 years of tradition behind it and it was created by a folk intent upon the workings of the inner man. Every possible physical response to emotion has been explored, isolated and docketed. Here we find the deliberate and the involuntary expressions of the face and hands deeply understood and technically taught. And this is reality in its truest sense, for it is the face and hands which betray to the watcher the emotions which have formed our lives.

She has drawn many of the other items from dances of Spain, Java, Japan, Hawaii and others.

La Meri : Performing Chathat, Arabic Dance

La Meri : Performing Pwe, a Burmese Dance

On dance compositions and choreography, she had written articles in 1954-55 and brought out a book on dance composition too.

She dealt with: (i) floor design, (ii) air design, (iii) music design, (iv) dynamics, and (v) dramatic design in this book. She also stressed on the topics of ideas, process, accessories writing out dance and group choreography. La Meri used simple sketches to illustrate floor designs.

She wrote her dance on easy-to-follow tabular columns. She often used Sanskrit terminology to describe the movements along with other special movements drawn from other dance styles. She also wrote out simple folk dances as shown in the appendix.

Traditional choreography like the Japanese theatre was adapted to an English-speaking audience by using a narrator (*sutradhara*) for heralding the actions performed on the stage. This she found was very effective in getting the attention and better appreciation from audience.

She had a long list of dances that she performed as a solo artist in various concerts. Beside that she had trained her Natya girls to perform many items hailing from different countries and choreographed them as group items. They had many invitations to perform in many places on many occasions. This programme was always well presented, varied and well appreciated.

The outline of the course material and dances will give an idea of the wide range of activities that the students went through and how well planned the whole programme was.

La Meri : Performing Echigo Jishi (Japan)

This was only possible because of the skilful pedagogy of La Meri and the hardwork put in by the teacher and students as well. Besides she gave detailed background of each country, dance style and its significance. She gave interesting assignments which enabled the students to acquire the knowledge and develop creativity.

An outline of her course content :

1. Geography and climatic conditions.
2. The people
   (a) Description
   (b) Characteristics
3. Type of music used in dancing.
4. Beliefs and customs concerned with –
   (a) Birth
   (b) Death
   (c) Marriage
   (d) Hospitality
   (e) Coming of age (boy, girl, both).
5. Religious factors affecting the dance forms.
6. Decorative arts (describe one).
7. Either five proverbs or five folk sayings that reflect the characteristics of the people.
8. One legend or myth related to dance or to characteristics of the people.
9. Describe one festival.
10. Describe the use of one dance. Give its name, its use in the customs of the country, its popularity.
11. Name one piece of fiction centered about the life of the country. Read the book.
12. State briefly the value of the above materials for exactive work.

OUTLINE OF COURSE MATERIAL

I. India, South (Bharatanatyam and Kathakali)

1. Music (*talas/ abhinaya/*verse forms)
2. Sculpture (Chidambaram, Ajanta and Elephanta)
3. Masks (and headdresses; Kathakali)
4. Costumes (*sari* and *choli; dhoti*)
5. Origins of racial characterisation, skills : kummi, folk dance.

II. India, North (Kathak and Marwari)

1. Music (talas and ragas)
2. Painting (Rajput and Mughal)
3. Costumes (*achkan, ghagra* and *chudidhar*)
4. Skills : folk dance *chittakas*

III. Japan (Odori)

1. Music (instruments; *Hayachi*)
2. Sculpture and painting (as it pictures dance)
3. Masks (*Kabuki* and *Noh*)
4. Costumes (*kimonos*, *obis*, etc.)
5. Skills : Folk dance

IV. Experiments in Oriental art forms

1. Java (Wayang Wong and Bedojo)
2. China (drama and the dance)

V. Experiments in Oriental art forms

1. Burma (Pwe)
2. Siam (dance drama)
3. Bali

VI. Experiments in Oriental art forms

1. Near East (Arabic influence)
2. Ceylon (devil dancers)

VII. Polynesia (Hawaii, Maori, Tahiti, Samoa)

1. Music (*Meles*, rhythms and percussion)
2. Sculpture (in racial history)
3. Masks (and facial painting)
4. Costumes (*malo, piu piu*, etc.)
5. Skills : *samoan, Sa-sa siva*

VIII. The Philippine Islands

1. Music (Spanish and Oriental origins)
2. Costumes (racial heritages)
3. Dance adjuncts (their significance)
4. Skills : salacot

IX. Spain, North and Central (Regional folk dances)

1. Music (folk instruments and their origins)
2. Sculpture and painting (as they reflect racial history)
3. Costumes (regional)
4. Skills : *muiniera*

X. Spain, South (Folk dances)

1. Music (Moorish influences)
2. Sculpture and painting (idea)
3. Costumes (regional and flamenco)
4. Masks (carnival, and their origins)
5. Skills : *el uyel dos*

La Meri : Performing Slendung, a Dance from Java

XI. Peru

1. Music (Inca instruments, rhythms)
2. Sculpture (Inca)
3. Masks (Inca)
4. Costumes (ancient Inca and modern)
5. Skills : *Huayno*

XII. Mexico

1. Music (origins : Aztec and Spanish)
2. Sculpture (Mayan and Aztec)
3. Masks (Idem)
4. Costumes (regional)
5. Skills : *chiapaneca*

XIII. Other South American Countries

1. Argentina
2. Brazil
3. Bolivia
4. Venezuela, Paraguay
5. Columbia
6. Chile
7. Ecuador

XIV. American Plains Indian

1. Music (melody line and rhythms)
2. Sculpture and painting (origins and significance)
3. Masks (dancing, masks and significance)
4. Costumes (as adjunct to dance)
5. Skills : wolf dance

XV. Africa

1. Music (melodies and rhythms)
2. Sculpture (sacred and secular)
3. Masks (ritual)
4. Costumes (regional)

As she grew older, she, being sensitive to the change in the dance world, felt the need to help the audience to be more understanding and appreciative and broad-minded. She also felt the great need to allow rich cultures and dance forms and artistes to influence each other for their mutual benefit and understanding.

Since one year ago I am refusing to teach Hindu dance to those who desire it for commercial purposes and the intimate secret I gave only to a chosen few whom I watch narrowly for any sign of defection in that line. For the past I can only ask pardon of Mother India for my weakness; for the future I shall behave differently. I want my studio to be not a school for manufacturing dancers, nor a clearing house for job hunters, but a mild sort of Ashram

La Meri : Performing an Arabic Dance

(retreat) for the student, for you. I want this place to help a little to strengthen ourselves in a moment when humanity so desperately needs strength.

The Ethnologic Dance Center grew out of the Natya School. During its opening in 1940 she said in her speech:

The ethnologic dance is the greatest travelling diplomat of the country it represents. East Indians never fail to thank me for what I am doing for India. Majority have no interest in the dance for itself, but they know that many persons came to study the politics of India because the unique dancer Shankar passed by and lit within them a spark of interest for his great land.

So here I am; the grim head of an ephemerous, idealistic thing called the Ethnologic Dance Center. The spiritual scope of it is a sort of good night for idea. We Americans are no pool in cultural background and there is so much we can learn in art and philosophy from other older peoples. 'Why from dancing?' you ask, 'Why not from books?' Because dancing is so much more direct, so much more honest, so much pleasanter. It is not the only way to get acquainted, but it is one of the best ways, and the one I am equipped to use and to teach others to use. (And right here I'd like to make a parenthesis. I believe that the U.S. as a race, is destined to turn out the best dance-artistes, just as Italy has turned out the best singers).

From a practical angle, the Center dreams of building many things to serve its idealistic scope of the brotherhood of man. We want first of all to build a public for the ethnologic dance. Building it, we will build the companies of artistes to satisfy this demand. And through these dancers with ideals who will not be forced into nightclub work. We have our one little company now, may it grow to be a big prosperous company; and then two, and then three. And our audience will be able to give great foreign artistes the understanding they deserve.

We hope and plan to make motion pictures of the great ethnologic dancers–Argentinita, Pilar Lopez, Shankar, Martinez. It is pretty dreadful to think that Argentinita died without leaving us the legacy of her dance, because Hollywood found she was not photogenic, and feared she'd be bad at box office.

We are striving to make this a Center where people from many lands may meet and become acquainted. We believe that only through mutual friendship can come world peace, and we are most anxious to give our mite towards that great end.

For her contributions to promoting ethnic dance forms, La Meri was awarded the Capezio Dance Award in 1972 and a Citation of the Texas Commission on Arts and Humanities 1973.

4

REFLECTIONS
Inspirations and Achievements

A long time ago there was one who said, 'There is no place for La Meri in New York'. For myself I have proved him wrong. There was a place, and I have filled it; in those fruitful years of giving, my own small cupful has added to the rising waters of my country's culture.

So many are gone; these friends, these creative geniuses of my generation. Never again shall we see the passionate, rhythmic pride of Argentinita nor the deep glowing beauty of Doris Humphrey. And even before them, Argentinita and Pavlova winged their lone flight into the mists beyond time. Yet it is not the partings which are the saddest, profound as they are but the waste of immortal beauty, the death of its envisioning. The incomparable Shankar, in his native India, with the shreds of his ideal school scattered about him. Juan Martinez, last of the masters of Spanish dance, struggling to pass his deep historical knowledge to the new youth. And beyond this lovely Tei-ko who never reached the accolade which was her right and who now sleeps beyond all hearing. And Maud Allen misunderstood for ever more because her lovely light was dimmed by the greater glory of Isadora Duncan.

Ruth St. Denis

Two unconquerable pioneers of dance in Americas, possessing the wisdom of long, unwavering dedication, have seen even greater changes come to pass than are yet known to us. These two are also my friends. I think I somewhat know their hearts, Ruth St. Denis and Ted Shawn. Martha Graham and Doris Humphrey have created new techniques so that the dancer may express himself unhampered by rigid rules.

Dancers faced many problems then and the younger ones continue to have more problems.

Uday Shankar

La Meri told them,

> Only your own hearts can tell you. Only you can find what facet of your timeless art will spark your inner self so profoundly that you will know, what truth in the words of Coomaraswamy, 'must' be said, and said clearly at all costs. Dance is also very demanding. It will not be possible to have a career in dance, and also what is labelled 'normal happiness'. To the true dancer, all of life is dance, all its experiences a reflection and enrichment of dance. I learnt by arduous stages that dance is its own pure joy. But if it brings sorrow, it is not the dance but the dancer who has for a moment falsified the art.

Her direct, warm and human approach in dealings with associates and students built up many relationships. Some of the interesting aspects of these relationships include these lines written by La Meri in her private diary.

> The highlight of the Paris dance season in the year 1932 was Shankar and Simkee. He was great, and personification of Shiva himself. It is he who taught Anna Pavlova Hindu dance. Although several Oriental names appeared on the concert roster that year, it is only one name 'Uday Shankar' that was worth recording. Uday Shankar brought to Paris audiences the beauty and sincerity of a spiritual experience for the first time. Shiva danced when he created the universe. Every gesture is laden with a meaning, even the uninitiated felt the rightness of the gestures without translation as the perfect sequence of moments melted into movements.

Uday Shankar inspired La Meri to learn Indian dance. She never forgot the moments that she spent with him. It will not be an exaggeration to say that it was he who gave her the impetus to become a serious dancer with a larger goal to work for. Allen Young wrote in the *Denver Post,* 'The backbone of his art is the culture and dignity of India presented with a simplicity which can reach every human being of whatever nationality'. Uday himself said, 'I always seek in my dance simplicity, power and beauty, and I think that is why my dances succeeded in having universal appeal, still remaining purely Indian without any influence of the West. All I did learn from the West was to avoid what was not India'. In an article he said, 'I have never claimed myself to be a classical dancer, though I have borrowed liberally from different styles through study and the cooperation of the best available teachers of the classical forms. And as for the West, I have certainly taken the best they could give us in discipline, presentation and showmanship for they have longer experience of the modern stage'.

In Delhi, I met Uday Shankar's wife Amala Shankar who recalled about La Meri, 'I remember the first time I saw her in Paris. I was only a young girl of 12. She used to come everyday and watch the rehearsals wearing a sari and she learnt various hand gestures and movements'. La Meri incorporated these into her class routine and called it the 'Shankar' exercise'. When Amala Shankar went to USA, La Meri arranged programmes for her and was protective about her. She admired Uday Shankar immensely and she wrote about him in her diary.

'Shankar', La Meri says, 'he himself is a personification of golden limbed Shiva and his inspiration springs from the richest of sources, sincerely and with absolute conviction in the heart'.

Ram Gopal hailed as Indian Nijnsky, son of Burmese mother and Rajput scholar, studied under Muthukumar Pillay and Meenakshi Sundaram Pillay. When La Meri came to Bangalore in 1936 he danced for her. She was impressed and asked him to join her troupe to travel all over the East. In the tour he danced solos and taught La Meri duets too. It is hinted that La Meri was jealous of his popularity and ditched him in Japan. The Polish critic Alexender Junta introduced him to Cecille B.-de Mille. He subsequently flourished as a dancer in Europe. He propagated classical Indian dance which was well choreographed and well presented.

Sunil Kothari* says, 'Ram Gopal owes much to La Meri. Working with her, he acquired considerable stage experience and learnt much about such matters as stage entries and exits, presentation, split second timing and lighting. Also about changing quickly and effecting quick-silver changes of moods and characters, for La Meri used to perform to 3-minute gramophone records of various countries'.

In her diary she wrote the amusing complaints made by Indians about Ram Gopal who had joined her troupe:

1. He looks like a Chinese.
2. They can't tell if he is a man or woman.

She added, 'My list of complaints is too long to write' but she penned a few:

(i) I surely will not be associated with Ram on any project short of a Broadway production where I handle only American kids.
(ii) The insincerity of Ram is appalling! He feels that only money is the answer to all the problems, and his childish lies and subterfuge are pathetic (when they are not irritating). He is so driven by this passion for (what ? social quality ?) and is so stupid in his efforts to get it, that he generally defeats his own ends. What has happened to his European prestige that he is driven to lick the Americans ?

These are her private thoughts which she never published. Ram Gopal in his book *Rhythm in the Heavens* also wrote about his meeting with La Meri:

I was at the Cantonment station seeing off a friend of mine on her way to Madras. Her train had left and I was walking back towards the exit. There was a tap on my shoulder. It was Mr Cooper, the Parsi who owned this so-called Opera House. 'Come and meet the dancer, La Meri'. We walked across and were introduced. A well-built women in her mid-thirties stood in front of me. Beautiful blue eyes and the figure of a tennis champion, an athlete. The most nasal drawl I had ever heard issued from her in a friendly greeting.

Daily after that, during her season at the Opera House in Bangalore I taught her all she ever knew of Kathakali, as she had never been to Malabar, and did not intend to go there, and preferred to learn, anyway, from me directly. Finally it was decided that after hearing her enthusiastic talk of her forthcoming Far East tour, my parents agreed that I could join her. 'Of course, you understand that you will not be paid anything. Your father can give you an allowance and after we reach Japan, by which time you will learn all there is to know of stagecraft, you will be paid a salary'. Those were the kindly words of encouragement I got from her Italian husband.

Perched high up on her loaded lorry full of costume trunks, to and from boats and stations, sweeping the stage, and helping to clean, put up and remove her black velvet tabs, these and

---

* A dance scholar and critic.

lots of other jobs were mine during that period of apprenticeship. We visited all the big cities in India and then from Calcutta went on to Rangoon, Malaya, Java, the Philippines, China and finally Japan. Everywhere I was studying the dances which this dancer attempted to learn.

'It's just a routine: I have a knack of picking up, notating and getting the proper costume,' she would say. In my opinion she completely ignored the spiritual and mental attitude and consequently her interpretations were more mental than 'under the skin' studies, authentic as they were.

In her Hindu numbers, we danced to 'canned' music. We got rave notices, as also did my solos 'Siva', 'Indra' and 'Peacock' Kathakali-styled dances.

It was an exciting lesson to watch La Meri put on her make-up, or should I say change her face with the flick of an eyebrow pencil and lipstick to suit the numerous characters she attempted to portray. I thought how intelligently and swiftly she changed. She was a Hula dancer one moment, then Spanish the next, and as quickly changed to Russian ballet technique. Now she appeared as a Mexican doing the 'Jarabe Tapatio' dancing on the brim of her hat, then she was Nijinski faun, a Marwari nautch woman, a Burmese belle, a Javanese princess, the Spirit of a lake, a mechanical straw doll, mechanical lifeless, still. I am only mentioning a few of her numbers. There were dozens more of these three-and four-minute 'numbers' that filled her seemingly inexhaustible repertoire of dances. I began to think as time went on, as we moved from country to country, that there was something very entertaining and clever about what she did and she did it with every ounce of conviction and sincerity of which she was capable. But I felt that if it took Pavlova of a lifetime to perfect one technique alone, as it did with Nijinski and Karsavina, and my great masters in India, how could any dancer attempt to present an 'Evening of the World's Dances?' (and she did it and with conviction).

Nevertheless, the first-hand experiences I had of watching, learning, working and suffering the most abominable discomforts compared to home all prepared me for the future. So many Indian dancers want the 'soft way' and imagine that fame, success and money pour in at the box office by the very fact that they have to just appear and dance and that they will get the 'red carpet' treatment from press and public alike.

La Meri also had a great respect and admiration for Balasaraswati whom she affectionately called 'Bala' for she represented an age-old tradition, namely a long vigorous training in Bharatanatyam, complete with mastery of mime technique and music and a lifetime devotion to the propagation of her unique art. 'Bala' performed in La Meri's institution and La Meri also arranged for her performances elsewhere and gave explanations about her repertoire. 'Bala' had a great respect and admiration for La Meri.

Gina Bleu or Srimati Gina as she was called, was a friend of La Meri. She came to India and studied Indian dances like Bharatanatyam and Kathakali. She performed in La Meri's institute and shared her knowledge of Hindu dance with her. She sent descriptions of the basic steps of Manipuri dance (Chali) to La Meri. She also performed in the festivals organised by La Meri.

Ibrahim Farrah who received the Ruth St. Denis awards, dedicated a programme in 1979 in Ethnic Dance Arts Inc. to La Meri,

A model for today's ethnic dancer in America. She has given us a sense of belief in our hard work. Even if at times things seem dark and development slow, we can look back at someone who has pushed and driven herself with endless belief in her art form. We can look to America's most outstanding ethnic dancer and scholar "the grand lady of ethnic dance".

People who studied under her had the utmost love and regard for her, as seen from some letters, written by her former students.

My brief association with you and your school has been a heart warming experience and one I shall look back on with nostalgia. In these days of strict commercialism, the presence in our midst of an institution like yours stands as a beacon to harmonious living and working towards a common goal and for the common good. Your reward in this world will not be measured in coin but in the happiness and pleasure you create with your work. Again I salute a great lady and a noble spirit. (From: Dan Gunio of Imperial Spirit Motion Picture Club, New York City.)

Mariano Para

Nala Najan was one of her close associates, who was living in the United States of America. He used to send bulletins to *Sruti* magazine published from Chennai till he died in 2002. In his letter dated 8 December 1967, Nala Najan wrote to La Meri from Italy, which throws light on La Meri's activities as well as his deep regard for her:

Mariano said you were worked up like hell up there and I am really sorry to know that after all these years, he is so stingy to you with La Loot. You have survived so many crises; that is a miracle when I come to think of it. I would certainly make sure he knows next season just what you will and won't do and for how much lira (this was a comment on Ted Shawn of Jacob's Pillow).

Nala Najan

I would love to rehearse for *Bach Bharatha* and work on the number you did for Julliard on Vivaldi. God knows you opened doors for me, in a thousand ways that I am still discovering. It's amazing how lasting an influence you are, my couperin, directly from the path you started with *Bach Bharatha,* etc. And so many other things, I do, think about and stage for myself. So you see La Meri dear, who can really measure the power for a word, the lasting influence of a work, a dance, it happens, it grows, it ferments, it inspires. Thank God again that I went to your school before I went to India; I realize this now more intensely than I ever did.

She had worked out a book with Nala Najan and gave him advice on how it should be put together. The book was titled *Primer of Indian Dancing.*

She had a lively and enquiring mind and that encouraged meaningful communications between her and her associate, age being no bar. Few excepts from letters written to her by her students, which express their love and respect for her as a teacher and friend, are reproduced below :

* * *

My Dear Dickie* [La Meri],

This is a so long wished for in-between letter, not one for birthday or Christmas but I have so very often wished to write you in-between times, but unfortunately never seemed to get around to. There is always so much to do, that one keeps promising oneself, tomorrow, tomorrow, tomorrow.

And now at long last I have two reasons that make this possible to have a little talk with you on paper. For one, we have had, and still have, a bad winter, with cold, snow, rain, and stormy winds—consequently I am indoors most of the time, and fewer of our friends drop in on us too because of bad weather. And secondly, I waited until I had finished your book *Dance Out the Answer* Dickie, so that I could tell you how I liked it. About two months ago I wrote to an old friend of ours in New York to buy and send me your book, which he did, but it took the post a month and a half to reach me. But, when at long last I got it, I practically devoured it.

Oh Dickie, I enjoyed it so much. You are a wonderful writer, and now I feel I know you so much better than I thought I already did—also dear Lillian, of whom through circumstances I really knew so little. My admiration for you, and for Lillian has grown so tremendously after reading your life story. I have always had you on a pedestal so to say, as an artist, as a human being, and as a beauty, and now my admiration and love for you have grown even more.

I hope you have the patience, and time, to read this long chat of mine Dickie? As for me, I am glad I had this little talk with you, especially as I am still full of your wonderful book, and wonderfully wonder you.

I will be writing you soon again dearest Dickie, and in the meantime we wish you the best of everything, and I mean everything.

We embrace you in thoughts, with our fond love, and a big kiss from each of us.

Collin & Jay

* * *

Most dear Dickie [La Meri],

You haven't asked me, but in planning for the future, you would probably like to know just where I stand. So I am writing it to you, in order to spare you at least one conversation on the painful subject, also a letter carries more weight than things said in the emotion of the moment.

---

* Dickie was a nick name used for La Meri by some of her friends & family.

As you know I am extremely fond of both of you and I wish more than anything to remain friends with you both. Though I have naturally heard more of one side than of the other, I am determined not to pass judgement (even to myself) or in any way to "take sides". If, as has been suggested, I have contributed to the present situation by out-staying my welcome in your home and thus throwing a spotlight on undesirable characteristics, I will regret it all my life, for I realise that I could never atone for such a thing. In that connection I can only humbly ask your pardon for my lack of insight and tact in not moving out long ago and trust that being such a fine person, you will one day forgive me. So much for the personal angle.

Artistically, I was enthused about you and deeply convinced of the value of your work, long before I met you. That conviction has remained unchanged and the enthusiasm has grown with the years. It has been a rare privilege indeed to be connected with this work, something I hoped but never dreamed possible when I first saw you dance at the Arts Theatre Club. You know how sincerely I appreciate your innumerable artistic and spiritual gifts to me, so I won't go into that again now.

Jo

* * *

Dear La Meri,

Writing to you always sends me into flurry of memories. Share a few with me.

I remember when I first came to you (not going on 14 but 15), I was all adoring and worshipful. I sat at your feet and looked up at you with a swelling feeling inside me.

I matured - and graduated to a chair. The feeling inside kept growing even larger.

When I became a woman (going on 19) I found it was time to steady myself on two feet (mine). So I left mama (that's you), and I was really busy facing the world on the slow - but - sure foundation you had given me. The feeling blossomed into some-thing rich and permanent. A love and gratitude for you I shall always have.

My love to Lillian and all.

Carol

There were many who benefited from her hardwork, knowledge and techniques. It is also heartening to note that many were touched by her open and friendly disposition. There may have been human feelings, like jealousy and personal prejudices in the earlier part of her life but she evidently grew out of this phase to become what she eventually became.

Original 'cygnets' in 'Swan Lake'

5

SPOTLIGHT
Stars on and off the Stage

La Meri was fortunately appreciated for her different qualities during her lifetime. Though she felt that her motherland (USA) was the least appreciative of her contributions, she did not get discouraged.

Few brief extracts mentioned below from a cross-section of personalities show, how La Meri was admired and commended for her multifaceted contributions in the field of dance. As a dance teacher, writer and promoter of ethnic dance, and dancer and probably more than that her various efforts to make ethnic dance and dancers a bridge to span cultures from far and near, La Meri was recognised by many.

Jack Cole

The Texan who achieved world fame as La Meri combined scholarly researched authentic dance with something like St. Denis creative imagination and performing flair. Perhaps the most potent image lingering from St. Denis early twentieth century American Orientalism is that of idealized self. La Meri's legacy to her modern pupils was her conception of dance as vehicles for showing change, rather than for describing status quo.

(Donsha and Madam Lurka who combined medical gymnastics with dance.)

The *Borzoi Book of Modern Dance* written by Margaret Cloyd Alfred mentioned that in 1949:

Two American orientalists have their influences on young Jack Cole and Hadassah. They were Ruth St. Denis and La Meri. They were presented at the Enthnologic Dance Center which is directed by La Meri alone. She hailed from Texas and was inspired by Mexican Latin American dances in her childhood, to devote her life to the study of Spanish,

Oriental and other enthnologic forms. She spent years in world travel both as touring dancer and scholar and considers India the matrix of the dance. She is essentially an educator, teaching and presenting the authentic forms in authentic costume, but of recent years she has been composing freely within these forms.

Her translations of the ballet *Swan Lake* and *Scherherazadi* into the Hindu idiom to their original scores have been novel and entertaining accomplishments. Her *Bach Bharata Suite* which adapts the classic Hindu movement to the classic western music in an abstract dance of singular beauty is even more interesting, for in it can be discovered certain basic movements that faintly resemble the movements of modern dance. La Meri is not a modern dancer but her explorations within the chosen field may yet indirectly sway some of the new directions the modern dance will take.

Ruth St. Denis

There has always been an Oriental undercurrent in modern dance, beginning with the occidentalised Orientalism of Ruth St. Denis, Oriental feeling of Mary Wigman and sometimes Martha Graham, Davis Humphrey and Charles Weidman could not escape the Oriental input in their dance development. She had many friends and admirers amongst her contemporaries who were authorities on dance or dancers of repute themselves. La Meri's multifaceted personality and talents and achievements are revealed by the reviews and comments made by these associates. Walter Terry was one with whom she had a long lasting interaction. He in his foreword to La Meri's book on total education in ethnic dance, said,

> My profound admiration for La Meri spans almost the entire length of my own career as a dance critic – that would be forty years. During those years, I have relished her dancing, been stirred by her experimental choreography on ethnic themes, savoured her wit and drunk thirstily of her incredible and endless knowledge of the world's most deeply rooted dances, ethnic dances. It is a superb book. The book is not a compilation of steps, patterns, routines. La Meri explores and explains the immeasurable importance of generation and flowering of ethnic dance. Yet she can depart from worldwide sweep and focus upon a single part of the body, in this case the spine and its unique place in defining ethnic dance charateristics. This chapter on the spine is one of the most brilliant and revealing chapters of a brilliant mind and uniquely informative.

Mohan Khokar in his book, *His Dance His Life* (A Portrait of Uday Shankar) says that, 'Shankar's influence among the modern dancers was pervasive but hard to pinpoint. After the war, a number of Americans influenced not only by Shankar but also by the choreographer, dancer and teacher La Meri, a force to reckon with no doubt, began to study Indian dance in particular Bharatanatyam, seriously and one of them was Jack Cole'.

In this connection, Khokar mentions that Jerome Robbins was strongly influenced by Indian dance as fostered in America by Shankar and others in creating the big dance drama in the musical *King and I.*

La Meri's tour to the Orient which she described as a thousand memories, through years weaving a tapestry that Marco Polo might have envied, created a deep impression on her mind and she felt that there was a great need for the students of ethnic dance to have information and instructions which would help them to understand the dance forms and to progress and evolve as an artist. Therefore she wrote the book *The Gesture Language of the Hindu Dance* with a lot of photographic illustrations. In her introduction she said, 'The hand language of India is as complete and expressive as any spoken language. I myself speaking no Tamil, have conversed with my teacher and colleagues by means of *hasta mudras*'. She also added, 'In many years of devotion to Bharatanatyam I have not found any book similar to mine. So it is my hope that these pages will fill a need and because of their very simplicity be an aid to better understanding of an art which has the power to give both performer and watcher an integrated strength of spirit which is unique'. This book was reviewed by W.G. Raffe, ARCA who wrote:

The Gesture Language of the Hindu Dance: Madame La Meri is a Kentucky lady who has given many years of study in what the archaeologists still call 'fieldwork'—on various forms of the art of dance, chiefly in Europe and India, and has divided her interest between ethnological aspects and securing instructions for her own actual performances in artistic public demonstrations; these have evoked considerable interest recently in New York among more serious students of the dance. In this new book she offers some account of her researches in India.

Madame La Meri therefore, journeyed to India and there found teachers who instructed her in practical work. Many photographs of these gesture poses are shown in the book here under review.

Certainly the principal value of this excellently printed volume resides in the generous array of unique photographs, especially made by Mr Carreras, and beautifully reproduced in collotype. They all show, without exception, the author demonstrating numerous poses, no less than 34 in *assamyuta* and 28 in *samyuta* form. She omits any detail of footwork and does not indicate the traditional *bhangas* which are so often evident in the God images. It is of course not possible to put every aspect of Hindu dance easily within one book.

Madame La Meri is, then, here concerned principally with dance as a living art, not purely Hindu despite her title, for she selects for exposition three main phases: the Kathakali pantomime drama of Kerala and Malabar; the Sadir Nautch, also of Southern India; and the Muslim-influenced dance mode we see in the Northern Provinces, the U.P. or the Punjab known as Kathak. From these three sources, she claims modern Indian dance is of epigrammatical contrasts; yet herself contradicts some of her definitions. She says, for example (in p. 5.[1]) that 'the occidental dance aims to excite; the Oriental dance to soothe'. But on her next page she writes: 'The Hindu theory is that the art of arts is to excite the imagination of the spectator to the emotion of imagined beauty' which is correct, but not necessarily soothing in its aesthetics.

Dance with masks

But the deep contrast mentioned, of *Natyadharma* as compared with *Lokadharma*, could well have been brought out with more detail and force. But Madame La Meri appears to have devoted far more attention to practical work than to reading. 'In many years devotion to Bharata Natya I have not found any book similar to this *The Gesture Language of Hindu Dance* of mine'.

It is true that not many books on Oriental dance do exist; counting even those known written in various Indian languages, they remain few. But is it possible that the author is unacquainted with the definitely parallel work on the *Ritual Mudras of Bali* by Tyar de Kleen? Though these *mudras* centre more on ritual than on dance, more on yoga than on expression, the fundamental alliance is close.

Madame La Meri's book will certainly be welcomed in all schools of dance; moreover, will find it of value for its fund of visual gesture. Much devoted labour has gone to its compilation, and in the United States it should do much to extend a wider comprehension of the aesthetics of the art of Hindu dance, especially with her continued practical demonstrations, calculated to awaken American interest in this beautiful art.

Of all the variegated happenings in the realm of the dance during those decades, only two more events shall be dealt with. They also stood out in a fundamental sense.

When Uday Shankar did his Hindu dancing in Vienna for the first time, it was neither more nor less than a veritable bewitchment. True, there was not anybody in the audience to understand properly and in detail this thrillingly exotic gesture language without the help of the printed comment in the programme folder. However, one definitely felt this was a full, rich and wonderfully articulated body language, a language, as it were, with a highly developed grammar and an exuberant abundance of the words, although all was so strange and different. And at any rate, the aesthetical and emotional enhancement and the general spiritual appeal worked perfectly.

The most startling and bewildering effect of Uday Shankar's performance was that it opened one's eyes to quite forgotten a truth: to the truth that on the other side of the crest of the mountain there is another valley. One got an inkling of the fact that the earth was indeed very big and that Europe was just a relatively small peninsular outgrowth of Asia, after all. And the idyllic, innocent not to say native, cultural solipsism of the white man, his conception as if this culture were the only one existing in the world, was somewhat staggered that unforgettable evening in Vienna.

This, was one of the two events mentioned. The other occurrence was still more extraordinary.

A matinee of Max Reinhardt's theatre in the Josefstadt was dedicated to the first dance performance in Europe of a young and entirely unknown American lady. This in itself was unusual enough and aroused curiosity. Well, that performance was thrilling and fascinating indeed. And yet, there remained an enigmatic, unsolved residue.

This lady produced a series of dances of quite diverse, heterogeneous foreign races. This alone would not have been so particular to be sure. It had happened again and again that a dancer inserted in her programme, to render it more variegated some piece or other of an exotic colour and flavour but this time it was different. This American lady danced a Chinese dance, an Indian dance, Hawaiian, American Andalusian Austrian dances, court dances of eighteenth century France, and so on. And all these pieces, so thoroughly different, were performed not only with a mastery of the various techniques and an obvious authenticity in every detail of the costumes, but, in addition with such a power of what appeared to be a transformation of the whole personality of the dancer that the onlooker was almost dumbfounded by such changeability, such an incredible liquidity and looseness of the ego complex of a human being. A desire arose and grew to see unveiled the true, own personality of this artiste. But this desire was not gratified. One felt oneself fooled somehow because it was so impossible to indicate which of all those transfigurations expressed her very self. And, after all, exactly this would be considered the scope of all genuine art; to unveil the artistes innermost self ? An art that counted had to be of the 'True confessions' type, so to speak. Did this lady consciously refuse making transparent her inner self? Was she too much of a lady and too little of an artiste?

Among the piece of that program there was one dance seemingly fitted for dispelling such suspicion. It was superscribed "Introspection" and its topic was just this quest for the real self. The dancer, supposed to symbolize the human soul in her fervent search of her true self, appeared with a mask. After a while of dancing, she pulled off the mask and fixed it on the dark curtain, but when she turned to the audience again, one saw there was still another mask hiding the genuine face. And so this play of unmasking was reiterated several times, until at length there emerged, symbolizing the unfettered self, the naked face, beaming with happiness over the freedom ultimately won after all those attempts at self cognition. By Jove, what a dance! This was profoundly philosophical, an outside metaphysical performance, soul-stirring to the utmost something like a danced comment on Heraclitus word: 'It is myself that I have been searching for'. And we felt, finally, this was indeed the "true confession", the revelation of the innermost craving of this astonishing lady artiste. We understood, she too, was seeking her real self. But at the same time, we still had the agitating impression that the true face of her own kept on being hidden, either because she had been, before us, replacing purposely just one mask by another in all instances throughout the whole performance, or because she had not yet succeeded in her own searching for her very self, for, strangely enough, not a single moment had we got rid of that stirring uncertainty, that puzzling inability to psychological identification.

And now I have to make a confession myself. Not perhaps the disclosure that the artiste I have been speaking of is La Meri. I bet you have grasped it at once anyway. What I have to avow today is something else. All that sophisticated guessing and conjecturing 12 years ago was wonderfully and very significantly wrong, and only now we can resolve that unsolved, enigmatic residue.

Of course, had La Meri scorned exposing her own inmost being and feeling? An all-round personality, a sterling artiste of an abundant inner richness, being a poetess, a musician and composer and a very great scholar as well as a dancer, La Meri just did not believe already at that time, in that western idea of emotional self-exhibition as being the essence of art. She had quite consciously adopted and put it in her book. But now should we have known that this young lady had already merged deeply into Eastern wisdom. And that her dancing was designed, also, to direct attention to the inexhaustible and fathomless spiritual riches of the East as a remedy against the gruesomely growing and spreading spiritual improverishment of the western world?

However, this message was not the only one of La Meri's to remain unnoticed at that time.

La Meri had been lending her artistic skill and her wonderful gift of expression to the dances of so many diverse and even thoroughly heterogeneous peoples and races with equal love and equal devotion, this, too, implied a message. By her ethnologic dancing La Meri had been preaching to all mankind all the time while travelling around the earth ball the golden, never fading gospel of human brotherhood.

Both of these messages – the first of which, by the way, is implied in the second – have become the leading ideas of this new institution. This Ethnologic Dance Center is La Meri's great contribution to the peace effort of mankind. She is convinced that "Should the divers folk of the earth be taught to know each other, they would automatically learn how to respect and love. Expression which communicates most directly and intimately the very nature of a people". She held that on propagation of this knowledge, the various folk dances are particularly apt to bring forth and promote a mutual understanding and brotherly love among the dwellers of this earth. La Meri hopes and faithfully believes – and so do you with her, I am sure – that this center will become a nucleus of an ever growing community of dancing missionaries of this cheerful creed.

(F. Cleve, an erudite art critic from Vienna)

On La Meri & Her Contributions

La Meri is doing a remarkable and unique work in using the dance as a means of interpreting peoples to one another. In every country the dance is perhaps the most spontaneous expression of the spirit of the people. To present dances from many countries beautifully and honestly, as La Meri does, is to bring together in unison and in contrast the likenesses and differences in our world.

Pearl Buck

La Meri, who had long ago, become a world-celebrity and by now also in her American homeland is past the point of being just discovered, is a unique phenomenon. There is nowhere on the Earth today, and there has never been in history, such a union of factual unbiased, authentic knowledge—gained at first-hand—of the various dance-forms of the people of the globe; with the complete capacity, not merely for learning these dance-forms, but also for performing them in an altogether artistic and compelling manner. It is no more than a bare statement of fact to say that such a personality has never existed in the Past, nor is its like to be found in the Present.

Felix Cleve

Your exposition and demonstration of the traditional dance of various countries, based on careful studies made with the help of indigenous masters, has not been limited to their merely aesthetic aspects, but extends to the content and raison d'etre, and is of great value accordingly.

A.K. Coomaraswamy

One of the greatest values of La Meri's approach to the dances of the Orient and of the Hispanic people is, paradoxically enough, that she is neither Oriental nor Hispanic herself, but a perfectly good North American. Her own basic movement instincts are thus the same as ours, and she is accordingly able to present the movement arts of alien peoples against a background that makes them increasingly intelligible to us. She speaks, as it were, our language as well as theirs, which makes her an ideal translator.

Jogh Martin

The future of the world depends on our knowing more about each other and on our developing mutual cultural and economic interests. The arts are the best bridge between peoples of different races.

Eleanor Roosevelt

In bringing the Indian dance so brilliantly to America, Madame La Meri has rendered a singular service, not only to the cause of Indo-American understanding, but also to the cause of cultural and artistic understanding between people and races of this globe which has shrunken so much that humanity cannot long survive unless yesterday's strangers develop the capacity to live as today's next-door neighbors. I have seen Madame La Meri execute Indian dances at her School of Natya, and I hope others will be thrilled as much as I have been.

Krishnalal Shridharani

Whenever I get to thinking of the fine creative scholarly work which La Meri is doing in her Center in New York City, and when I reflect how really few creative artistes teachers there are in America who add definitely to our sum of true culture, I want to rebuild the Government so that she can have real support to carry on her work. That's the way I feel about La Meri and her international labor for beauty.

Ruth St. Denis

We who strive to foster the American dance should be ever grateful to La Meri, for she has brought to us many treasures from the world's storehouse of dance. These treasures are not merely museum pieces, but rather are they vivid and vital contributions to our own theater of dance and rich nourishment to our growing, but still immature, systems of dance education. To La Meri, then, is due unstinted praise for her gifts to dance, for the gifts and the giver deserve the support of all those who want for America a varied, emotionally exciting and intellectually stimulating dance.

Walter Terry

The Shawl Dance

6

RAINBOW
The Colourful Life and Beyond

One after another I have flung joys and sorrows into the lake of life, watching them give to the water their prismatic colours. Like many others choosing this course I have sacrificed prodigally to remain true to my choice. The one man I could love wholly and with appreciation after the breaking of an unhappy marriage, came to me so late that it was too late to amalgamate with the world of which by my choice, I was forever a part.

La Meri writing out the chronology of her life said,

"A whole life...and a very long and very full one. And I have been rewarded with good health and a lot of happiness" and she quoted from *Bhagavad Gita*, chapter. III:

verse no.		8	–	Action is superior to inaction.
"	"	9	–	Perform action without attachment.
"	"	25	–	The wise should be devoid of attachment, being desirous to help mankind.

When one achieves my years, one can be objective even about oneself. As a dancer I had something special...an instinctive anatomical ability to catch work over into my creative group world. I also have good instinct for music, both eastern and western. As a teacher I care more for motivation than technique...thus I turn out dancers, not technicians.

These abilities were recognised by every teacher abroad with whom I studied, and in every country in which I danced. Except my own. I have long ago passed the point of personal irritation about this brush off by my own country. What is a continual irritation is the fact that this attitude slows down the work I would like to accomplish. In 1940 an eminent critic said that there was no place for La Meri in New York. I can be grateful that there have been a number of young students who did not believe him, but who worked with me, and thereby realized a career of their own.

For 30 years I have ploughed through a sea of obstacles from simple misunderstanding and bitchy remarks to sheer unethical dirty work. But I say "To the dancer, the stage becomes the entire universe and by the magic of her mimetic skill, through the dance of the hands and eyes, she creates and portrays in her performances the abode of the gods, the descent to the lower regions of the demons, the beauty and profuseness of nature and the joy and sorrow, humor and ethos of man". This brief time on stage represents for the dancer the peak of achievement, the end result of each prosaic day finally merged into this day this moment, the now, the dance, this Dance, of Life?

La Meri presents Nala Najan with 1981 Ruth St. Denis Choreographer's Award

It is over, the dance ends, the curtain closes. Slowly I begin to remove the costumes, make-up, ornaments. The skill and endurance required to carry one through the vigorous patterns of movement demand from the body all the energy and strength it is capable of exercising. As each muscle and nerve relaxes after having been taxed and stretched to its capacity, a feeling of lassitude, of sheer physical relief and utter relaxation steals over one as the body returns to its normal state. And with this pleasurable sensation comes the satisfaction of knowing that the beauty one had been seeking all of one's life has been realized.

With the daily routine of living and functioning in the world around us comes a higher manifestation of consciousness a complete realization of one's humanity in which the individual maintains a dialogue of love with all created beings, projecting oneself to meet and understand them.

A little seed sown can become a bush forest with more varieties of trees in it. Similarly a good intention and good education can influence a large and ever expanding circle of humanity. They individually spread their wings and the message and goal of La Meri. To give an example in the EDA newsletter dated February 1976, the alumnae news said:

"Cindly Maddox is on tour with Luis Rivera and returns to go on tour with Bhasker. Jean Mellichamp has returned from two months engagement in Spain, Cynthia Small is teaching Spanish Dance in Boston, Barry Edson is staging a ballet, Amelie Hunter graduates from UCLA this spring, majoring in Indonesian Dance. William Adams and Paula Johnson danced in New Bedford for the American Field Services".

Matteo

As the needs and circumstances kept changing, La Meri made new efforts to

La Meri : the Teacher

continue with her life's goal. Ethnic Dance Arts Inc., a dance company presented the first all professional festival in July 1970. It was an unique organisation exclusively devoted to ethnic dance. Its activities peaked in 1974 and slid down rapidly due to various problems. In these festivals, she presented many distinguished dancers from different countries. Amongst them were Bhaskar, Rita Devi, Manjushri Chaki Sircar, Govind and Ratilekha from India. But La Meri managed to run it till 1980. To encourage dancers working in the field of ethnic dance and choreography, she started the Ruth St. Denis awards. In 1981 this award was given to Nala Najan at a function in New York which was taped. In her hearty southern drawl she gave a short speech and said perhaps this would be her last 'Rumba' in New York. Others who received this award were Jean Mellichamp in 1977, Bhaskar in 1978, Ibrahim Farrah in 1979, Mariano Parra (her adopted grandson) in 1980.

In 1982, EDA offered Ruth St. Denis award in competition. Awards were also won by Sacko Ichiniohe (Japanese), Carolyn Kay (East Indian), Jane Goldberg (Tap) and Teo Morica (Spanish).

La Meri's special talent lay in her ability to watch for crucial distinguishing body-movements, gestures and moods which characterised different special dance styles. She learnt through analysis of these features, by trial and error. She distinguished herself as an excellent teacher, choreographer, writer and promoter of dancers and dances.

Her life was a continuous adventure in dance, full of vigour and persistence; she never gave up under pressure, nor compromised for monetary reasons, nor was untrue to her deeply-felt artistic convictions. Even though many of her friends and admirers are no more, her technique and spirit continue to endure in the works of many of her pupils all around the world.

OBITUARY

LA MERI (1898-1988)

Described as 'The undisputed queen of the ethnic dance' by Walter Sorell, the dance writer, La Meri was long considered the leading American authority on the subject, particularly the dances of India and Spain. She toured the world at the height of her career, in the 1920s and 1930s studying and performing in South and Central America, Europe, Scandinavia, Africa, Australia, New Zealand, Tasmania, India, Burma, Malaya, Java, the Philippines, China, Japan, Ceylon and Hawaii.

La Meri made her professional stage debut in 1924 in San Antonio, where she danced prologues to silent movies. In New York, she performed with Maria Montero and was a featured vaudeville performer with Keith Time and in the 1949 Broadway revue *A Night in Spain.*

La Meri wrote six volumes of poetry and five books on dance aesthetics, technique and composition. Her extensive collection of material on ethnic dance, given to the New York Public Library in 1948 and 1962 is a major holding of the Library's Dance Collection. In 1972, La Meri received the Capezio Award.

The New York Times.
January, 1988
By Jennifer Dunning

* * *

La Meri renowned ethnic dancer, choreographer and teacher, died January 7 in San Antonio, Texas, at the age of ninety.

Her early interest in East Indian dance was kindled by a performance in Paris by the late Uday Shankar, who became a lifelong friend. La Meri went on to become the first westerner to study East Indian dance in India, where she was taught by Papanasam Vadivelu Pillai, Srimathi Gauri, and Ram Dutt Misra. Among other teachers during her performing career were Michio Ito, U.P.O. Sein, Ratharana, Soerharsono and Jose Otero.

La Meri was a close friend of Argentinita and her sister Pillar Lopez, and at Argentinita's behest, she began teaching at Jacob's Pillow in 1942, where she remained as resident teacher, performer, and choreographer for eleven years. La Meri's teaching launched the careers of a number of ethnic dancers, among them De Falco, Matteo, Mariano Parra, Nala Najan, Jerane Michel and Rebecca Harris.

Dance Magazine, *April, 1988*

APPENDICES

1. Professional Training
2. School of Natya
3. Books Written
4. Stray Leaves — The Star Roper
5. Research Material on "La Meri" — In the New York Public Library for the Performing Arts, Lincoln Centre, New York
6. The Ethnolo0gic Dance Center
7. The Dance Programme at Columbia University

Appendix 1

PROFESSIONAL TRAINING

San Antonio, Texas	1913-201	Studied ballet, Spanish and Mexican dancing from local teachers
Hawaii	1917	Hawaiian dance from Ana Hila
Barcelona	1922	Spanish dance from Dona Paulina
New York	1925	Ballet from Tomaroff and Tarasov; Modern dance from Michio Ito
Mexico, D.F.	1926	Mexican dance from Fernandez
Buenos Aires	1928	Argentinian dance from Rodriguez
Venezuela		
Colombia		
Panama, Peru, Chile, Paraguay	1928	Studied from local dancers
Sevilla	1929	Spanish dance from Otero
Granda	1929	Flamenco from La Bisca and Gitanas
Fez	1929	North African dance from Fatma
Paris	1931	Ballet from Volinine; Hindu dance from Uday Shankar
North Africa	1932-34	Studied from native dancers
Wakawarewarewa	1936	Maori from Bella and Rangi
Kandy, Ceylon	1936	Devil dances from Ratharana
Madras	1936	Bharatanatyam from Papanasam Vadivelu Pillai and *abhinaya* from Srimati Gauri Ammal
Lucknow/Lahore	1937	Kathak from Ram Dutt Misra
Rangoon	1937	Pwe from U.P.O. Sein
Batavia	1937	Srimpi and Bedojo from Soerharsono
Tokyo	1937	Odori from Yeichi Kudera
Manila	1937	Local dances from Tolentina
Honolulu	1937	Hula from Juanita
Santiago	1938	Cueca from de Garnham
Buenos Aires	1939	Flamenco from Carmen de Toledo

Appendix 2

SCHOOL OF NATYA
Various Phases of Progress

Founded—May, 1940 by Ruth St. Denis and La Meri at 66 Fifth Avenue, New York.

15 MAY 1940 TO 1 SEPTEMBER 1941

APPEARANCES

Studio Recitals, Lectures—35; Ruth St. Denis and La Meri at Kaufman Auditorium and W. Irving Auditorium; Various recital-lectures in and around New York.

WORKS CREATED

Devi Murti; *Krishna-Gopala*; *Gauba's Journey to Paradise*; 50 various ethnologic dances.

1 SEPTEMBER 1941 TO 1 OCTOBER 1942

School moved to Master Institute at 310 Riverside Drive, New York.

APPEARANCES

Master Institute— 6 concerts and 6 lectures.

CONCERTS

Barbizon-Plaza (sponsored by the India League); Guild Theatre; Washington Irving High School; Waldorf (East & West Association); Bosten Symphony Hall (East & West Association); Tour of New England. Shavitch Opera Company (June); Jacob's Pillow Dance Festival (3 concerts, July); Season at Hunterton Hills Playhouse —20 performances.

WORKS CREATED

Ea mai Hawaiinuiakea; *Caudro Flamenco*; *Surpanakha in Love*; many short dances.

15 OCTOBER 1942 TO 5 JULY 1943

Ethnologic Dance Center founded by La Meri at 5 East 46th Street.

GUESTS OF HONOUR

Pearl Buck; Dr Lin Yutang; Ruth St. Denis; Argentinita; Sarkis Katchadourian; Ted Shawn; Krishnalal Shridharani; J.J. Singh; Dr Henry Zimmer; Dr Felix Cleve; Dr Marguerite Block.

APPEARANCES

Studio Recitals and Lectures—17; Short tour of New England; India Independence Day Dinner; three concerts, Barbizon-Plaza; Unity through the Dance Concert; Benefits in and around New York; Jacob's Pillow Dance Festival.

WORKS CREATED

Fireflies by Tagore; Burmese Dance Suite; Chinese Dance Suite; Moroccan Dance Suite; *Rama Breaks the Bow* (Japanese Wayang-Wong); *El Amor Brujo* (concert arrangement); Polynesian Dance Suite.

8 JULY 1943 TO 1 APRIL 1945

Ethnologic Dance Center at 110 East 59th Street, New York. (studios formerly occupied by Isadora Duncan and later by Ruth St. Denis).

APPEARANCES

Studio Recitals and Lectures—74; Museum of Natural History—10 concerts; Cortland State Teachers College; International Woman's Exposition, Madison Square Garden; Manor Club—Allentown Concert Forum; Jacob's Pillow Dance Festival.

WORKS CREATED

Urmya; Rig Vedic Hymn (Dance Suite); *Episodes on the Life of Buddha* (Created by Gina); *Dances of Aragon* (Dance Suite); Latin-American Dance Suite; *Swan Lake* (in Hindu Dance Idiom to music from Tshaikowsky); *Fl Amor Brujo*; *DeFalla* (full ballet); Near Eastern Suite; Indian Dances; Animal Dance suite; Story Dance suite; Percussive Dance Suite; Hymns and Spirituals; *Alborada Del Gracioso* (Ravel); Tagore's *Chitra* (full drama); Two Polynesian Dances; Two Caribbean Impressions; *Scheherazade* in Hindu Dance Idiom (Rimsky-Korsakov).

Appendix 3

BOOKS WRITTEN BY LA MERI

ON POETRY

Poems, privately printed, San Antonio, 1917.
Marching to France, printed by Army Y.M.C.A., 1918.
Mexican Moonlight, Cornwall Press, Boston, 1920.
Poems of the Plains, Richard Badger, Boston, 1922.
The Star Roper, Dorrance and Co., Philadelphia, 1924.
The Star Roper, Special edition, Sunset Press, New York 1928.
Songs and Voyages, privately printed, Leghorn, 1938.

(Poems in prominent poetry magazines in 1918-28; also in Braithwaite Anthology, Literary Digest, etc., were also published).

ON DANCE

Principles of the Dance Art, Channing Press, London, 1933.
Dance as an Art-Form, A.S. Barnes, New York, 1933.
Gesture Language of the Hindu Dance, King's Crown Press (Columbia University) N.Y.C., 1941. Second edn., Blen Press, N.Y.C., 1966.
Spanish Dancing, A.S. Barnes, N.Y.C., 1948. Second rev. edn., Pillow Press, 1967.
Dance Composition, Pillow Press, Massachusetts, 1965.
Gesture Language, (Second Edition), Blen Press, N.Y.C., 1966.
The Spanish Dance
The Technique of the Hindu Dance
Dances of Many Lands

CONTRIBUTED ARTICLES TO THE FOLLOWING

Dictionary of World Literature
Dance Encyclopaedia
Dance has Many Faces
Encyclopedia Brittanica Book of Knowledge
Encyclopaedia American
Encyclopaedia dello Spectacele
Indian Arts & Letters

Articles... *Dance* Magazine, *American Dancer, Dancing Times* (London), *Home & Abroad* (Paris), *Harper's Bazaar*

WRITINGS ON LA MERI

Who's Who in the Dance World (London, 1932)
Dancer's Almanac (N.Y.C.) 1940.
Women of Achievement (New York, 1940)
Le Danja a Le Danja (Rome, 1940).
Invitation to the Dance Terry, New York, 1942.
Art of Hindu Dance..., Chatterjee, India, 1945.
The Dance (John Martin...1946)
Teatre de Hey (Merria Y Campos, Mexico, 1941)
Who Knows & What...Marques Co., Chicago
Let's Meet the Ballet (Samachson...New York)
Student Dancer Woody.

Appendix 4

STRAY LEAVES
The Star Roper
[A Poem by La Meri]

I'll throw my noose on a mustang star
And if my loop falls true
I'll strap a surcingle over his back
And we'll buck down the moonlit blue.

And if I can break him to ride him right
So he'll know my hand on the rein
And will answer my whistle and heed my voice
From a toss of his star-dust mane.

Then the Pegasus horse from his silver wings
Can travel, for all I care,
On the white north wind to Parnassus top
And trumpet the high, thin air.

For I'll ride my star to eternity's end
and the music of the spheres
Shall echo in tune of his silver hoops
For the staves of a thousand years.

I wrote the above little verse in the middle twenties when poetry was very popular in this country. My *Star Roper* was reprinted in many magazines. I wrote it about the time my childish ambition to be a cowboy was giving place to a slightly more mature ambition to be a poet and writer...So much for youthful ambitions! As it turned out, I could not have picked a wilder mustang to ride than the one branded 'ethnic dance'. But somehow I have managed to hang in there, and it is consoling to know that my star's hoof-bears will indeed mingle from those of the sweeping remnda of Indian and Spanish dance which will forever gallop down the centuries – La Meri.

Appendix 5

RESEARCH MATERIAL ON "LA MERI" In the New York Public Library for the Performing Arts, Lincoln Centre, New York

1. *Dance as an Art-form, Its History and Development*, La Meri (Pseud.), New York, A.S. Barnes and Co. Inc., 1933, p. 198, 20 cm.
   Bibliography : pp. 189-90, NN 71-518501 LC
   33-36025 (MGR)
2. 'The Dance West and East in Contrast' MGZA, *Dance Periodical,* East Strondsburg, Pa. [etc.], March 1941, p. 18, illus
   NN 70-380958
3. 'Dancing in India', La Meri (Pseud.). London, India Society 1939, p. 16, 28 cm. cover title, *Indian Art and Letters*, Vol. 13, no. 1.
   NN 71-518284 {MGS (Hindu)}
4. Tchaikowsky's *Swan Lake* in the idiom of the Indian Dance (n.p., n.d) p. 15, 31 cm. Essay on the creation of La Meri's *Swan Lake* and the Blending of Eastern and Western styles in dance and music –
   NN 73-7028755 {MG (Swan Lake)}
5. 'Why did I ever become a dancer', MGZA Dance Magazine, New York, Dec. 1950, pp. 16-17, illus.
   NN 70-147564
6. 'La Meri, Dancer for the Nations', Allen, Patricia Shirley, MGZA, *The American Dancer*, Los Angeles [etc.] March 1938, p. 11, 42 illus, parts.
   NN 70-286493
7. 'Flight Beyond the Horizon from La Meri', Bassoe, Henriette, MGZA, *The American Dancer*, Los Angeles, April 1941, p. 11, Port.
   NN 71-309205
8. 'Feet of La Meri', *Newsweek*, (New York, March 4, 1940, p. 39)
   NN 71-347926
9. Hering, Doris, Reviews La Meri's *Little Show*, December 5 1955, Brooklyn Academy of Music (New York), MGZA Dance Magazine, New York, February 1956, p. 11.
   NN 70-154862

10. 'The Miracle that is La Meri', Matteson, Olivia Baldessarelli, MA *Southwestern Musician*, Dollas, December 1951, pp. 16-17, 19, 30, 32 Ports.
NN 71-238595

11. India's Dance in America, Narghis, Shirada, MGZA Dance Magazine, New York August 1945, pp. 10-11, illus.
NN 70-110113

12. Orthwine, Rudolf. A new type of intimate dance theatre. All photos by Gerda Peterich (In : {MGZA Dance Magazine, New York, Nov. 1943} p. 17 illus). The erstwhile studio of the late Isadora Duncan and Ruth St. Denis is made into a new dance theatre by La Duncan Meri and Guido Carreras.
NN 70-78656

13. 'Eastern Dances for Western Dancers', Ram Gopal, MGZA, *The Dancing Times*, London, October 1962, p. 16.
NN 70-42980

MOTION PICTURES

1. (La Meri) (Motion Picture) 1948-51, 16½ m.m. si. b&w. 16 m.m. reel. 393 ft. filmed by Carol Lynh at Jacob's Pillow. Performed by La Meri.
Contents - Chethal at Maharma, 2 Hawaiian dances, 5 Hindu style dances. NN 72-7011950 (MGZHB 4-366).
2. (La Meri) (Motion Picture) 1948-51 15½ m.m. si b&w 16 m.m. si. b&w, 16 m.m. 1 reel 378 ft. filmed by Carol Lynh at Jacob's Pilow 73-7044608. (MG2HB 4-365).
3. (Rebecca Harris) (Motion Pictures) 1956 9 m.m. si. b&w from colour sequences 16 m. 1 reel 217 ft. filmed by Carol Lynh at Jacob's Pillow.
NN 73-7035065 (MGZHB 4-379).
4. The Seasons (Motion Pictures) 1960, 23 sd. b&w 16 m.m. 1 reel 828 ft. Vivaldis season performed at Julliard School, New York 1960
NN 73-7046246 (MGZHB 8-1072).

Appendix 6

THE ETHNOLOGIC DANCE CENTER

The Ethnologic Dance Center was founded in May 1940. During its first year, twenty-five lectures on various aspects of ethnic dance were presented to the public.

In 1941, continued lectures and performances (from a group of artist-students) rapidly built a public for the ethnic dance. By 1942, many very eminent people had become interested in the work being done. Ananda K. Coomaraswamy, Pearl Buck, Lin Yu-tang, Krishnalal Shridharani, Henry Zimmer, Felix Cleve, Ted Shawn, Sarkis Katchadorrian, Marguerite Block, Grant Code, Asodata Dafoa and Ruth St. Denis gave of their time and talent to further the work.

In July 1943, the E.D.C. moved to its present location in the studios originally built for Isadora Duncan.

In 1946, the Center presented the Young Artists Series, twenty-five fine young exponents of ethnologic dance, in New York debuts at the Ethnologic Theater.

New works from a truly pioneering scope were being continually presented. Guest artists were introduced in the Theatre and guest teachers gave courses in ethnic forms. By 1947 demands for out-of-town appearances had become so great that La Meri formed the Exotic Ballet Company to tour the States.

In 1947, the Center offered, for the first time, a certificate upon completion of the full academic course, thus establishing a school where the serious student may obtain not only technical instruction, but also learn the cultural backgrounds and practical aspects of the art.

The Center has created an audience for ethnologic dance, and sent out many fine young artists to serve that audience. It has also established the ethnic dance as the third of the dance-art triumvrate—ballet, modern and ethnic.

Appendix 7

THE DANCE PROGRAMME AT COLUMBIA UNIVERSITY

COLUMBIA UNIVERSITY
in the City of New York
SUMMER SESSION 1941
McMILLIN ACADEMIC THEATRE
FRIDAY, AUGUST 8, 8:15 P.M.
Dance Recital
LITIA NAMORA
Assisted by
EXPERIMENTAL GROUP OF SCHOOL OF NATYA
Courtesy of La Meri

Lucille Peters	*Evelyn Kraft*
Deirdre	*Mera Goorian*
Carolyn Hector	*Marian Jinishian*
Juana	*Iris Whitney*

PROGRAM

Invocational (South India) .... *The Group*
Saivic Puja (Bali) .... *Litia Namora*
(A Balinese Priestess executes a ritual to the God, Shiva)
Street Dance (Burma) .... *Litia Namora*
Yako San (Japan) .... *Lucille, Mera, Deirdre, Evelyn, Juana, Carol*
Slendang (Java) .... *Litia Namora*
Bhajinnas (North India) .... *Litia Namora*
Kathak Talas (North India) .... *Juana, Carol, Deirdre, Lucille*
a. Bola (three sequences)
b. Gaths—The Ball - The Kite
c. Bola (three sequences)
d. Gaths—Radha-Krishna - at the Well
e. Ektal (four counts against three)
Marwari Street Dance (North India) .... *Litia Namora*

INTERMISSION

Dance of the Gandharvas and Apsarasas .... *The Group*
(The celestial nymphs and musicians attendant on Parvati)
Maha-Devi (South India) .... *Litia Namora*
Four Aspects of the Goddess Deva
Shringara Rasa (erotic mood) .... *Parvati, the Wife*
Karuna Rasa (compassionate mood) .... *Uma, the Mother; Sati, the Faithful*
Veera Rasa (heroic mood) .... *Durga, the Militant*
Raudra Rasa (terrible mood) .... *Kali, the Destroyer*

INTERMISSION

Harem Dance of Salutation (Arabia) .... *Litia Namora*
Ouled Nail (Morocco) .... *Litia Namora*
Seguidillas Manchegas (Spain) .... *Juana, Carolyn, Lucille, Deirdre, Evelyn*
Bulerias (Spanish Gypsy) .... *Litia Namora*
Serenata (Granada) .... *Litia Namora and Group*